G000253766

Phonics and Spelling

Ages 6–7

Julie Crimmins-Crocker

Published by Collins
An imprint of HarperCollins*Publishers*
77–85 Fulham Palace Road
Hammersmith
London
W6 8JB

**Browse the complete Collins catalogue at
www.collinseducation.com**

© HarperCollins*Publishers* Limited 2011, on behalf of the author
First published in 2007 by Folens Limited.

ISBN-13: 978-0-00-745234-7
5

British Library Cataloguing in Publication Data
A catalogue record for this publication is available from the British Library.

Managing editor: Joanne Mitchell
Layout artist: Neil Hawkins, ndesignuk.co.uk
Illustrations: JB Illustrations; Bob Farley of GCI; Helen Jackson, Nicola Pearce and Peter Wilks of SGA; Colin King; Tony Randell and Leonie Shearing c/o Lucas Alexander Whitley.
Cover design for this edition: Julie Martin
Design and layout for this edition: Linda Miles, Lodestone Publishing
Printed and bound in China.

Contents

This contents list provides an overview of the learning objectives of each puzzle page.

Tips for parents

 Read through the title, introduction and instructions for each puzzle to ensure your child knows what to do.

 Point to the phonemes and words covered in the puzzle.

 Demonstrate what the phonemes and words look like and sound like.

 Let your child practise saying the phonemes, blending the phonemes and saying the words in each puzzle.

 Relate the phonemes to other words they know, for example, items in the classroom and at home that also have the same phoneme, rhyme, first phoneme, last phoneme and so on.

 Give your child practise writing the phonemes using a range of materials, for example, sand, whiteboards, crayons, paints and Plasticine.

 Let your child practise writing the phonemes 'in the air' and with pencil and paper, ensuring correct pencil grip and sitting posture.

 Provide additional support if your child needs it, by filling in letters and/or more challenging words/answers.

 After each puzzle go to 'What's next?' (see page 4) and cross off the completed activity. Let your child choose the next one.

Synonym: the same or similar meaning, for example, *big – large*.

Antonym: the opposite meaning, for example, *big – small*.

Anagram: the word is muddled up, for example, *GREAL – LARGE*.

Informal: the word is simple or slang, for example, *rabbit – bunny*.

Verbs are action and 'doing' words, for example, *run*, *talk* and *think*.

Nouns are naming words, for example, *pen*, *hat*, *apple* and *school*.

Adjectives are describing words, for example, *small* bird.

Adverbs add more information to verbs, for example, He ran *quickly*.

Phoneme: a letter or letters that create a single sound when said aloud, for example, **TH** and **OO**.

Letter string: a collection of phonemes, for example, **ELL**.

Vowels are the letters **a**, **e**, **i**, **o** and **u**.

Consonants are the letters of the alphabet which are <u>not</u> vowels.

What's next?

Use the words in the puzzles you have done to complete these activities.

Activity	Puzzle title	Date
Practise your handwriting. Write each phoneme or word five times in your book.		
Practise writing the words and then draw a picture for each one.		
Find three more words that begin with the same phoneme. For example, *cap, cat, cut,* all begin with **c**.		
Find three more words that begin with the same blend of phonemes. For example, *flag, flip, flop,* all begin with **fl**.		
Find five more words that end with the same phoneme. For example, *cat, hit, but, wet, net,* all end with **t**.		
Find three more words that end with the same blend of phonemes. For example, *fast, fist, post,* all end with **st**.		
Find three more words that rhyme.		
Sort the words into alphabetical order and put them in a list.		
Put the words into sentences. Remember to start with a capital letter and end with a full stop.		
Put the words into sentences that are questions. Remember to start with a capital letter and end with a question mark. For example, *Where is my cat?*		
Find opposites (called **antonyms**) for the words and write them in pairs or groups. For example, *big – small*.		
Sort the words into groups with the same number of syllables.		

Know your phonemes

Blend the phonemes to read the words. Circle the phoneme in each word that is the same as the phoneme in the star. One has been done for you.

Star	Words
b	(bed) rub black
c	cat cut club
d	dog bed drum
f	fox fat flag
g	go bug green

Star	Words
h	hen hat hop
j	jam jog jet
l	leg ball clap
m	mop jam plum
n	nut hen run

Know your phonemes

Blend the phonemes to read the words. Circle the phoneme in each word that is the same as the phoneme in the star.

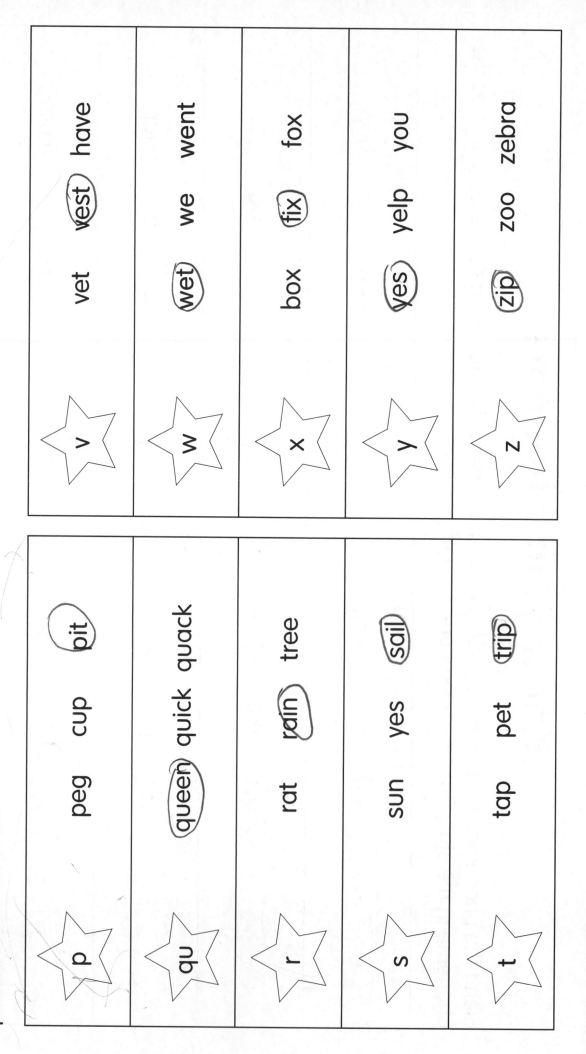

☆ p	peg	cup	(pit)
☆ qu	(queen)	quick	quack
☆ r	rat	(rain)	tree
☆ s	sun	yes	(sail)
☆ t	tap	pet	(trip)

☆ v	vet	(vest)	have
☆ w	(wet)	we	went
☆ x	box	(fix)	fox
☆ y	(yes)	yelp	you
☆ z	(zip)	zoo	zebra

Know your phonemes

Blend the phonemes to read the words in each rocket. Circle the phoneme in each word that is the same as the phoneme in the star. One has been done for you.

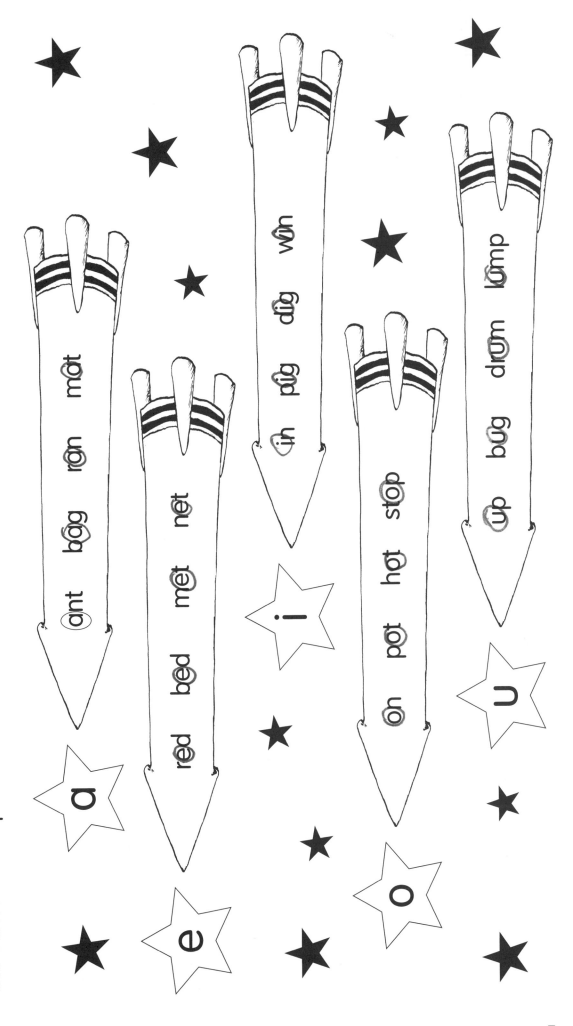

Alphabetical order

Write the missing letters in the footprints so that they are in alphabetical order. The missing letters that you need are in the spaceships.

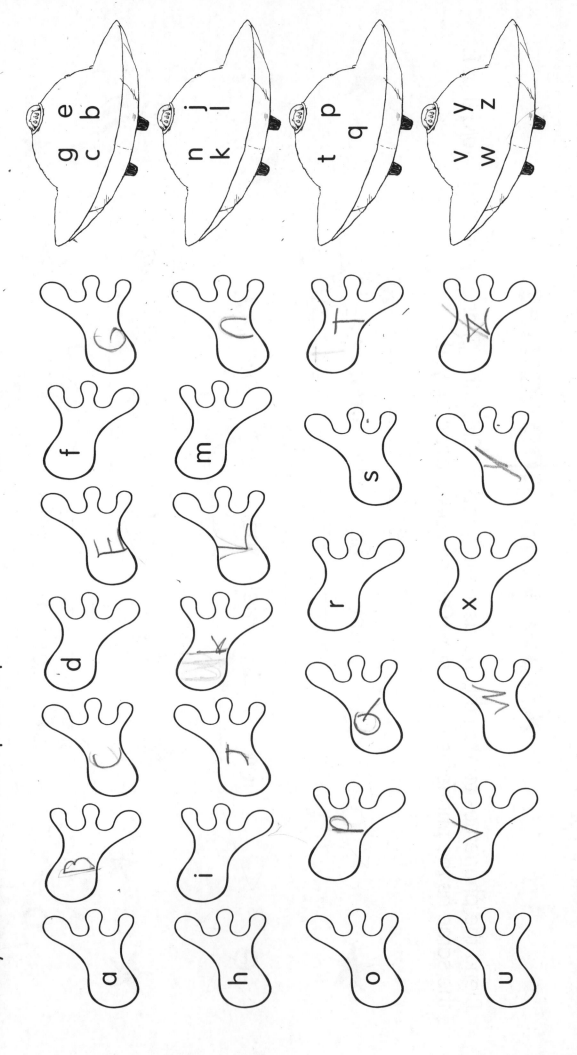

Alphabetical order

Put these letters into alphabetical order and write them in the stars.

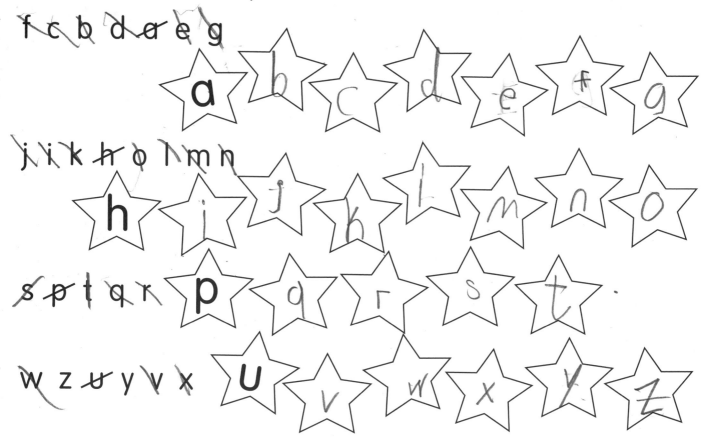

f c b d a e g

a b c d e f g

j i k h o l m n

h i j k l m n o

s p t q r

p q r s t

w z u y v x

u v w x y z

Fill in the gaps in the alphabet alien snake. The missing letters are in the stars.

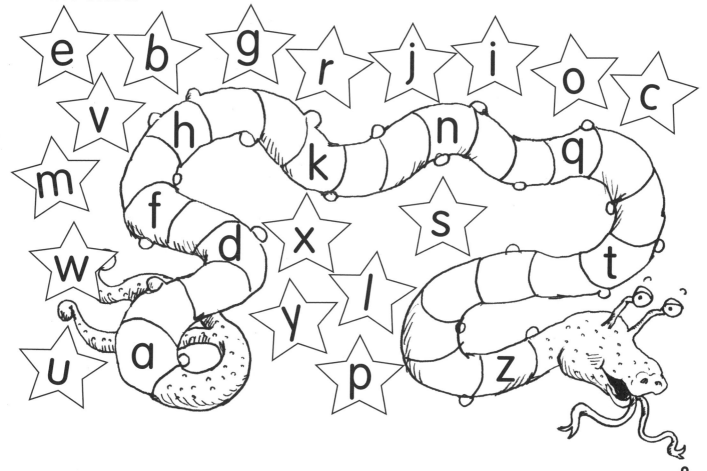

Alphabetical order

Look at the letters in each alien's hot-air balloon. Can you say each letter? Add the letters that come before and after it in the alphabet. Use the letters in the basket to help you. The first one has been done for you.

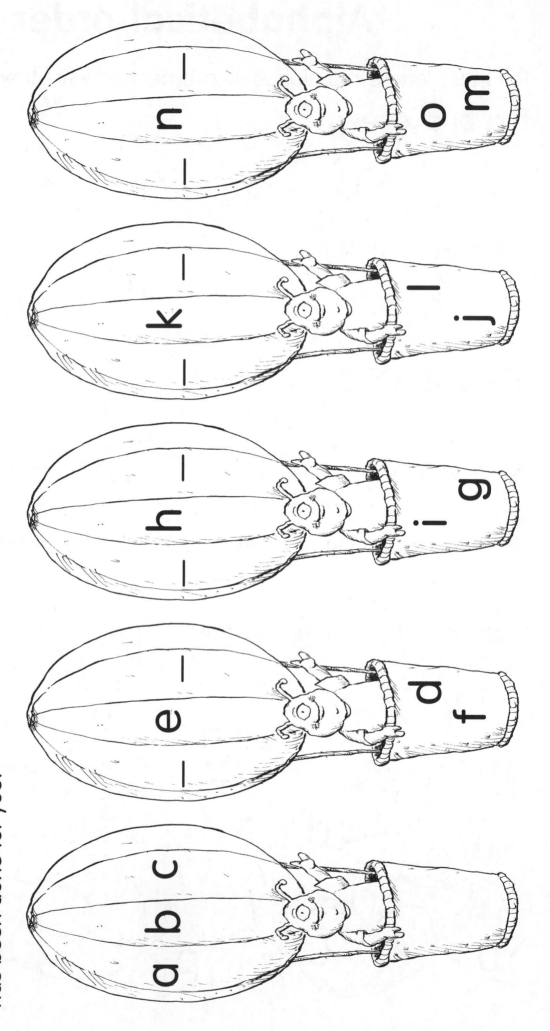

Alphabetical order

Look at the letters in each alien's hot-air balloon. Can you say each letter? Add the letters that come before and after it in the alphabet. Use the letters in the basket to help you.

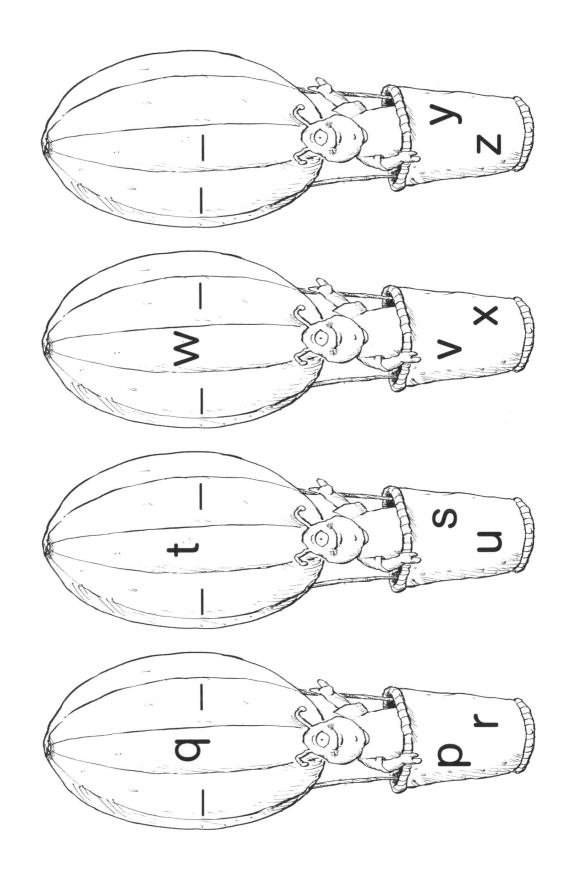

Alphabetical order

What can the aliens see out of the window of their spaceship? Join the dots in alphabetical order to find out. Some letters have been joined to help you.

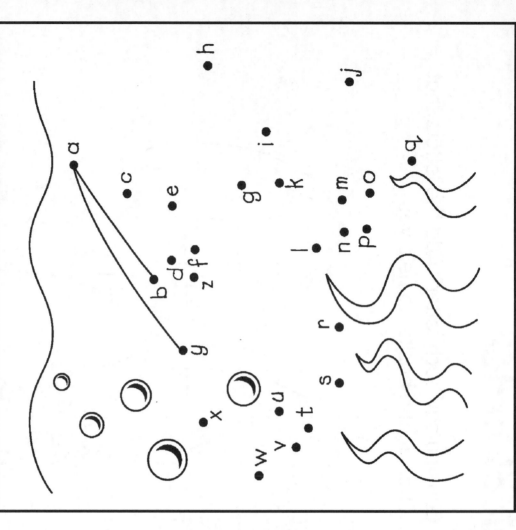

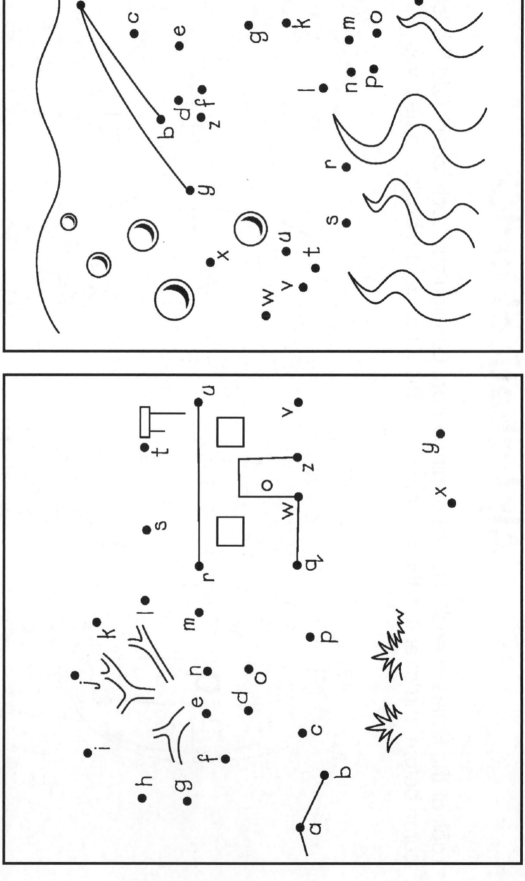

Alphabetical order

What can the aliens see out of the window of their spaceship? Join the dots in alphabetical order to find out. Some letters have been joined to help you.

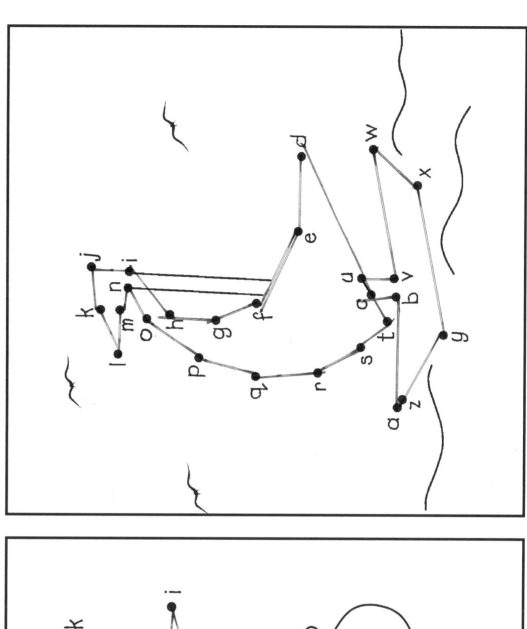

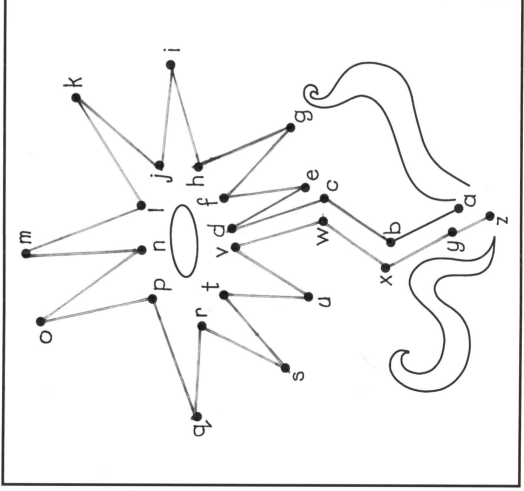

Alphabetical order

These words and pictures are in alphabetical order from A to Z. Write the missing phonemes of the words that are next to the pictures.

ant	_b_ ed	_c_ at	dad	egg	_f_ ox
gate	_h_ en	ice	_J_ ug	kite	_l_ eg
_m_ ap	nut	one	_p_ in	queen	rib
_s_ ix	_t_ en	_u_ mbrella	vest	_w_ eb	x-ray
_y_ acht	_z_ ip				

Alphabetical order

These words and pictures are in alphabetical order, but the letters are jumbled up. Unjumble the letters and write the words on the lines.

apple	tba ____	puc ____	dad	egg	anf ____
girl	ath ____	ice	jam	king	leaf
omp ____	ten ____	oil	peg	queen	tra ____
three	ugly	stev ____	giw ____	x-ray	yacht
			nus ____	zoo	

Words that begin with bl, cl, fl, gl, pl and sl

Blend the phonemes to read the words. Join the phonemes and write the words on the lines. Cut out the pictures and stick them next to the words.

b + l + ow = *blow*

c + l + aw = *claw*

f + l + a + g = *flag*

g + l + ue = *glue*

p + l + u + g = *plug*

s + l + u + g = *slug*

16

Words that begin with cr, dr, fr, gr, pr and tr

Look at the pictures and say what they show. Can you hear the phonemes in the words? Cut out the phonemes in the planets and stick them underneath the pictures to spell the words. You must use phonemes from each planet to make a word. Blend the phonemes to read the words.

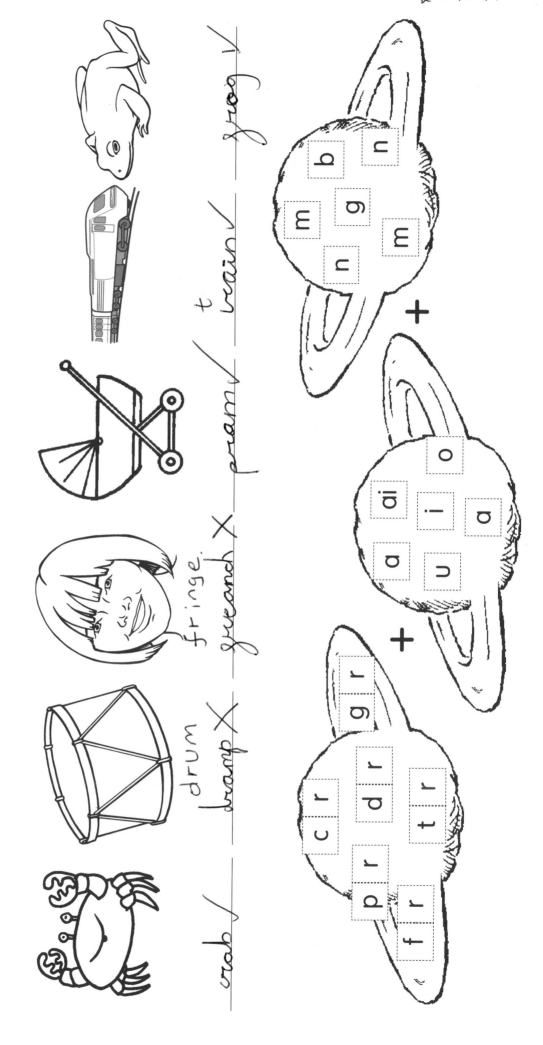

crab ✓

drum
tramp ✗

fringe.
greanch ✗

pram ✗
train ✓
t

frog ✓

Words that begin with dw, sw and tw

Look at the pictures and say what they are. Circle the words hidden in the wall. Join them to the pictures.

12

Words that begin with sc, sk, sm, sn, sp and st

> Read the sentences. Circle the words that begin with **sc**, **sk**, **sm**, **sn**, **sp** and **st**.

★1 The cut on my leg left a bad scar. ✓

★2 I like to skip to keep fit. ✓

★3 Some flowers smell nice. ✓

★4 A good card game is snap. ✓

★5 It is very rude to spit ✓

★6 The bus stop is next to the shop. ✓

Look at the blends in the helmets. Write the words that you circled above on the lines next to the correct blends. One has been done for you.

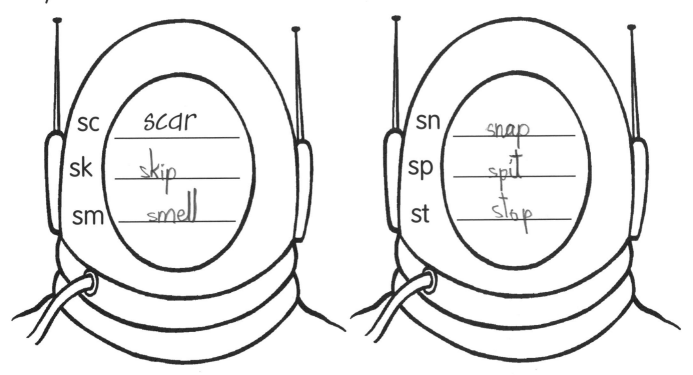

sc ___scar___

sk ___skip___

sm ___smell___

sn ___snap___

sp ___spit___

st ___stop___

Words that begin with two phonemes blended together

> Read the sentences. There is a word missing from each sentence. Blend the phonemes to read the words in the boxes. Cut out the words and stick them in the correct sentences.

⭐1 My cut began to [bleed] . ✓

⭐2 Mud is [brown] ✓
   pretty

⭐3 I like strawberries and [cream] ✓

⭐4 He was a funny [clown] .

⭐5 Catch the ball, don't [drop] it. ✓

⭐6 Birds can [fly] . ✓

⭐7 My painting had a red [frame] ✓

⭐8 The fire began to [glows] . ✓

⭐9 My plant [grew] tall. ✓

⭐10 The princess was [pretty] .

bleed ✓	✓
pretty ✓	✓
glow ✓	✓
fly ✓	✓
clown	✓
frame ✓	
brown	✓
grew ✓	
drop ✓	
cream ✓	

10/10   Well done!

20

Words that begin with two phonemes blended together

Blend the phonemes to read the words in the word bank. Can you hear the first two phonemes?

Word bank

scar	sniff	slow	small	sky
spade	try	twins	steep	sweep

step

> Highlight the words from the word bank in the wordsearch. The words can be read across and down.

t	s	n	i	f	f	m	l
w	z	s	t	e	e	p	l
i	l	s	m	p	t	l	s
n	s	p	v	j	m	d	k
s	m	a	s	l	o	w	y
k	a	d	q	t	r	y	x
h	l	e	s	w	e	e	p
r	l	n	s	c	a	r	c

Words that begin with ch, sh and th

Blend the phonemes to read the sentences and the words in the rockets. Choose the right word to complete each sentence and write it on the line.

⭐ 1. I ___chew___ food with my teeth.
My dog likes to ___chase___ cats.

chase   chew

⭐ 2. I put the tins on the ___shelf___.
The ___shop___ sells ice creams.

shelf   shop

⭐ 3. I said ___thank___ you for the gift.
The old dog was very ___thin___.

thank   thin

⭐ 4. After my swim, I had a hot ___shower___.
The sun made a big ___shadow___ under the tree.

shower   shadow

⭐ 5. My ___cheeks___ were red with sunburn.
Our teacher writes with ___chalk___.

chalk   cheeks

Words that begin with scr and spl

Blend the phonemes to read the letter strings in the rockets. Join the parts together and write them on the lines. The first one has been done for you.

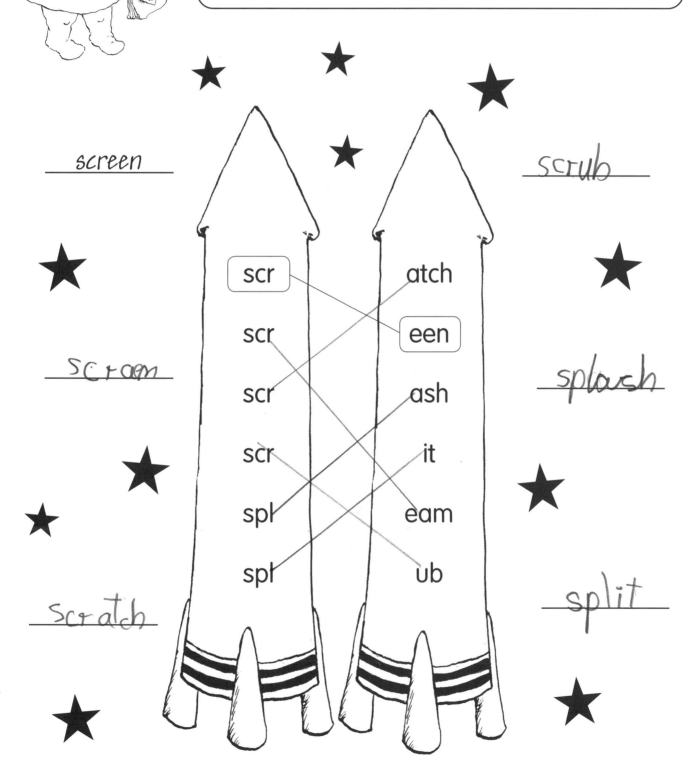

screen

scrub

scr — een

scr

scr — atch

scream

splash

scr — ash

scr — it

spl — eam

scratch

spl — ub

split

17.3.19

Words that begin with
spr and squ

Look at the pictures in the balloons and say what they show. Blend the letter strings in the feet of the aliens to read the words. Write the words in the aliens. Join the aliens to the correct balloons.

spring

square

spray

squirt

spr　ing　squ　are　spr　ay　squ　irt

Words that begin with str

Look at the pictures and say what they show. The phonemes in the words are jumbled up. Sort them out and write them in the boxes. Each word begins with **str**.

| t | s | r | aw |

| s | t | r | aw |

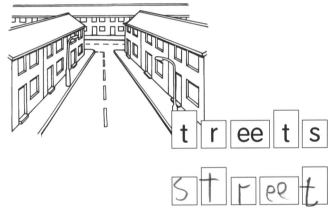

| t | r | ee | t | s |

| s | t | r | ee | t |

| i | r | t | n | g | s |

| s | t | r | i | n | g |

| t | r | n | g | s | o |

| s | t | r | o | n | g |

| r | s | aw | t | e | b | y | rr |

| s | t | r | aw | b | e | rr | y |

| s | e | t | r | t | ch |

| s | t | r | e | tch |

25

Words that begin with scr, spl, spr and str

Look at the pictures and say what they are or what action they show. Can you hear the blend at the start of the word? Choose the missing blend from the footprints and write it in the boxes in the rockets. Write the words on the lines.

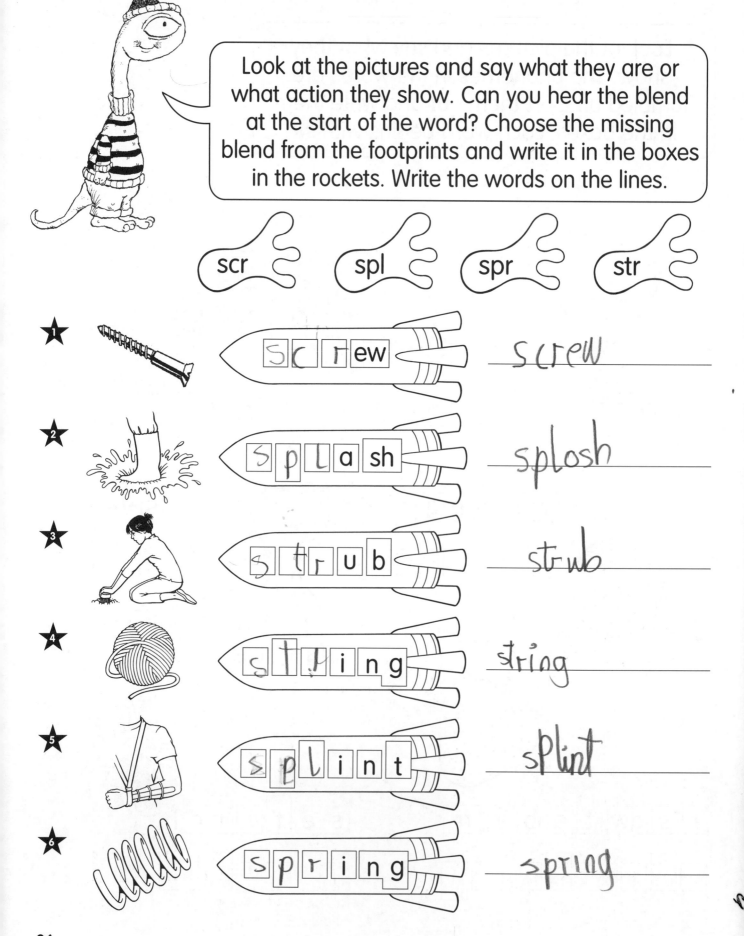

scr   spl   spr   str

1. ⭐ s c r ew — *screw*

2. ⭐ s p l a sh — *splosh*

3. ⭐ s t r u b — *strub*

4. ⭐ s t r i n g — *string*

5. ⭐ s p l i n t — *splint*

6. ⭐ s p r i n g — *spring*

Words that begin with thr

Look at the pictures in the leaves and say what they show. The phonemes in each snails' shells spell the words. Write them on the lines and join each snail to the right picture.

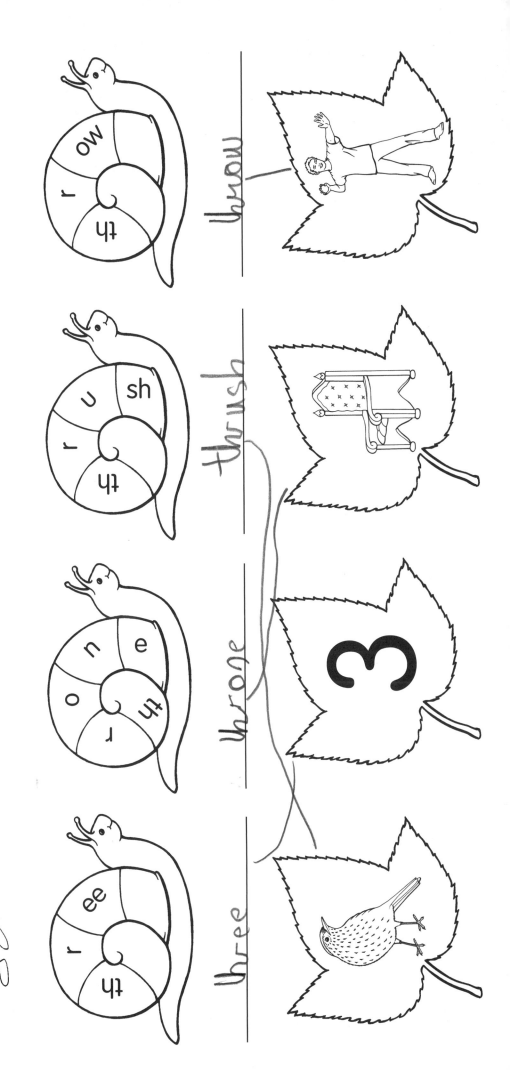

th r ow

throw

th r u sh

thrush

th o n e r

throne

th r ee

three

Words that begin with thr and shr

Blend the phonemes to read the words. Break the words up into phonemes like the example. Remember, some phonemes, such as **th** and **sh**, are spelt with more than one letter.

Example: throat ———→ | th | r | oa | t |

thrill ———→ | th | r | i | ll | ✓

thrush ———→ | th | r | u | sh | ✓

throw ———→ | th | r | ow | ✓

three ———→ | th | r | ee | ✓

shrub ———→ | sh | r | u | b | ✓

shriek ———→ | sh | r | ie | k | ✓

shrug ———→ | sh | r | u | g | ✓

shrink ———→ | sh | r | i | n | k | ✓

3

Words that begin with scr, spl, spr, squ, str and thr

Blend the phonemes to read the letter strings in the planets. Now read the sentences below. Add a letter string from the planets to complete the missing word in each sentence. The first one has been done for you.

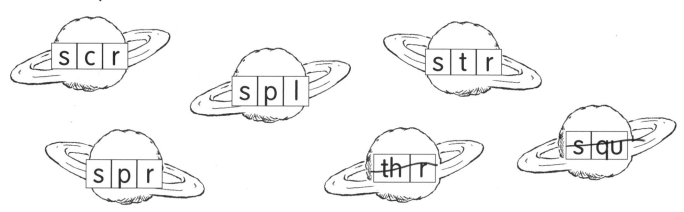

⭐ 1 I had a small | s | c | r | a | p | of paper to write my name on.

⭐ 2 The | s | t | r | a | y | dog had no home.

⭐ 3 We had to | s | qu | a | s | h | the clothes into the small case.

⭐ 4 The fish were in the | s | t | r | ea | m |.

⭐ 5 I had to | th | r | ea | d | the needle to sew.

⭐ 6 I | th | r | ew | the ball into the net.

⭐ 7 He had a | s | p | l | i | n | t | er | of wood in his finger.

⭐ 8 She jumps up and down as if she is on | s | p | r | i | n | g | s |.

⭐ 9 I | s | p | r | ea | d | the jam on my toast.

⭐ 10 The mouse made my mum | s | c | r | ea | m |.

The blends ch, ph and wh

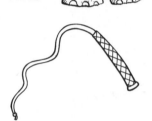

Look at the pictures and read the words to say what they are.

Christmas

photo

whip

Can you hear the phonemes at the start?
Look at the way they are spelt.

ch says **c** or **k**   **ph** says **f**

wh says **w**

Blend the phonemes to read the words below.
Find and circle the **ch**, **ph** or **wh** in these words.

white   elephant   when

chorus   whip   wheel

whale   photo   telephone

Words that rhyme

Blend the phonemes to read the words on the planets. Some of these words rhyme. Help the aliens get back to their spaceships. Colour the words that rhyme with the shaded word to show them the way.

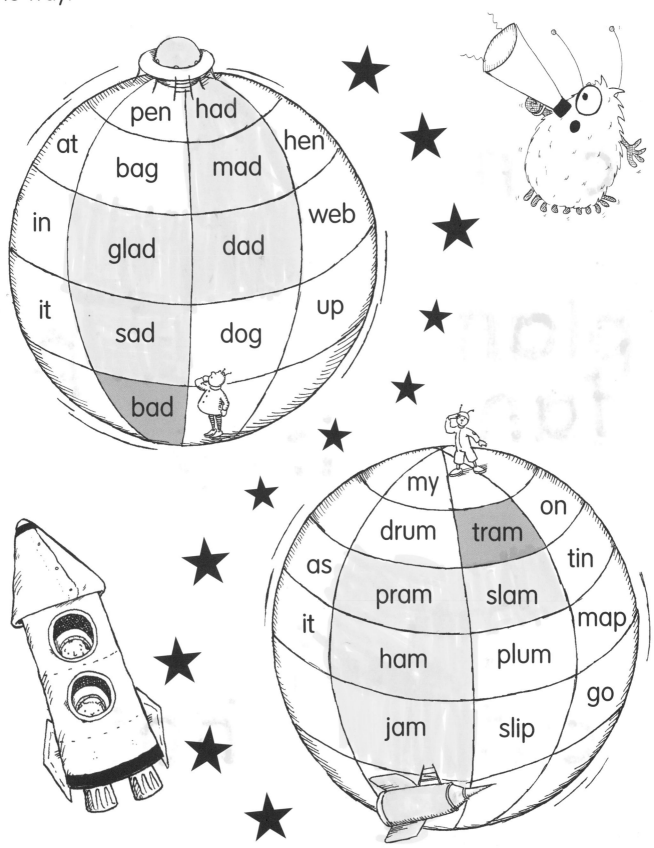

Words that rhyme

Blend the phonemes to read the words. Can you hear the words with the same middle and end phonemes? These words rhyme. Colour the words that rhyme in each group.

can
nut
plan
fan

clap
rip cap
trap

hat
cat flag bat

Words that rhyme

Blend the phonemes to read the words in the rockets. Can you hear the words with the same middle and end phonemes? These words rhyme. Join the words that rhyme from left to right. The first two words have been joined for you.

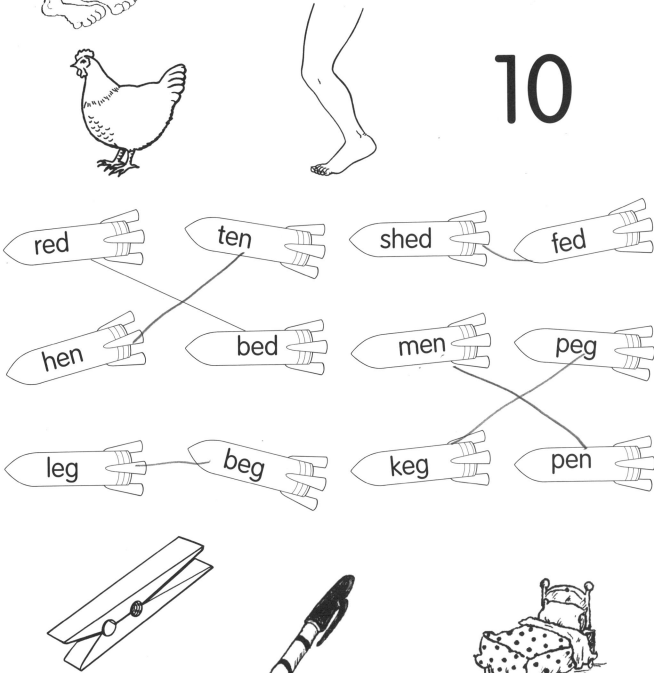

red	ten	shed	fed
hen	bed	men	peg
leg	beg	keg	pen

Words that rhyme

Words that rhyme have the same middle and end phonemes. For example:

h	a	t

c	a	t

d	o	g

l	o	g

Use a phoneme from each rocket with the i in the planet to make words that rhyme with the blends in the stars. Write the words on the lines.

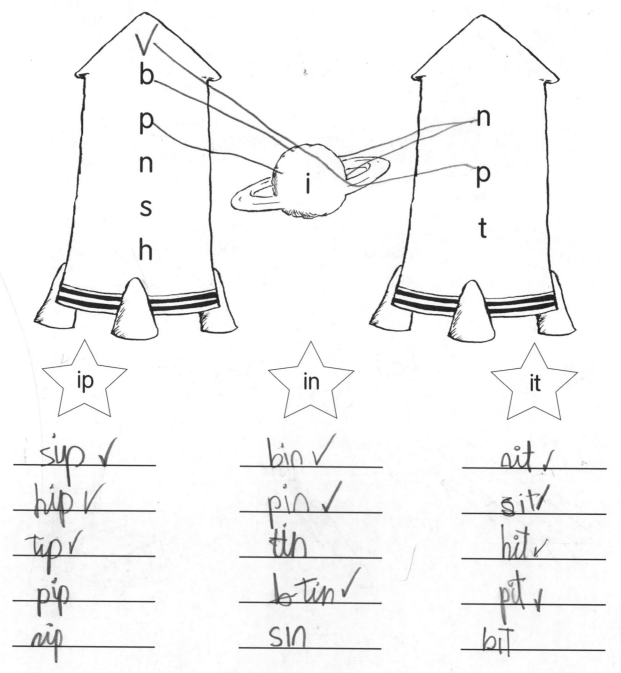

ip	in	it
sip ✓	bin ✓	ait ✓
hip ✓	pin ✓	sit ✓
tip ✓	tin	hit ✓
pip	b tin ✓	pit ✓
nip	sin	bit

Words that rhyme

Look at the pictures and say what they show. Can you hear the words with the same middle and end phonemes? These are words that rhyme. Write the first phoneme of each word. Join those that rhyme to the stars in the middle.

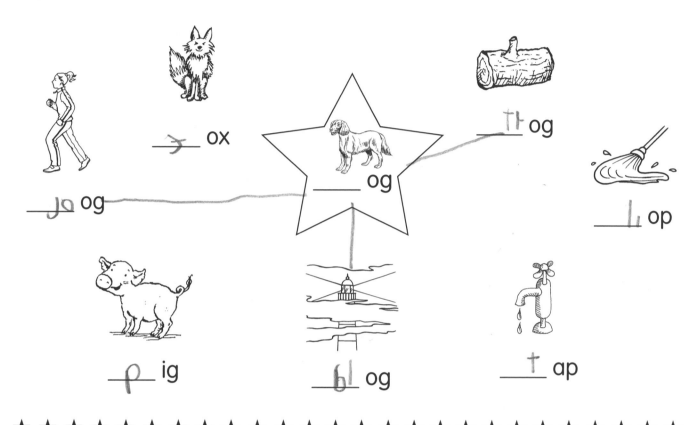

j ox

_fr_ og

_jo_ og

___ og

_l_ op

_p_ ig

_bl_ og

_t_ ap

★ ★

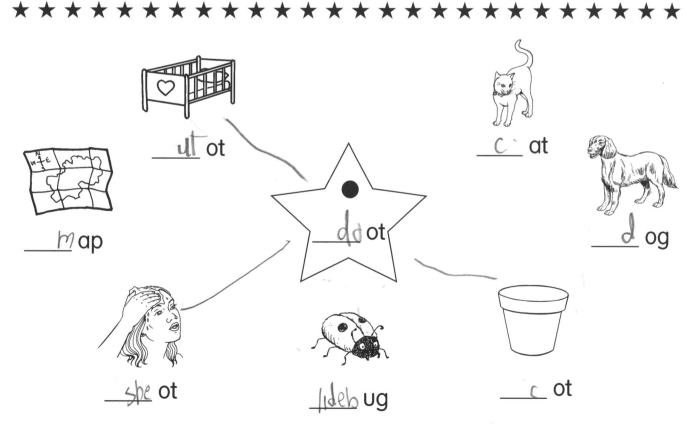

_ut_ ot

_c_ at

_m_ ap

_do_ ot

_d_ og

she ot

lideb ug

_c_ ot

Words that rhyme

Write in the middle and end phonemes. Blend the phonemes and say the words. Circle the pictures that rhyme with the word in the star.

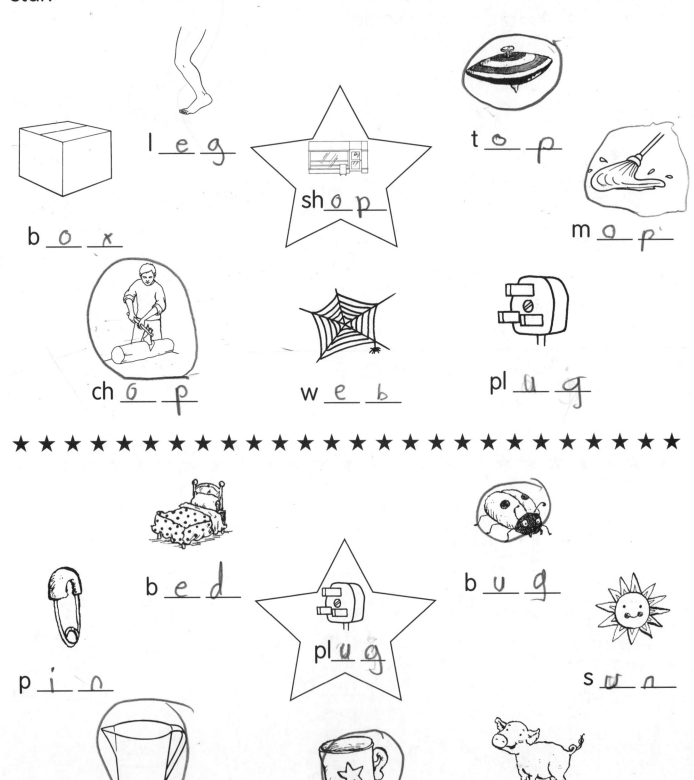

l e g

t o p

b o x

sh o p

m o p

ch o p

w e b

pl u g

★ ★

b e d

b u g

pl u g

p i n

s u n

j u g

m u g

p i g

Words that rhyme

Look at the pictures in the stars and read the word. Can you hear the middle and end phonemes? Cut out the words at the bottom of the page. Stick the words with the same middle and end phonemes in the spaceships next to the pictures.

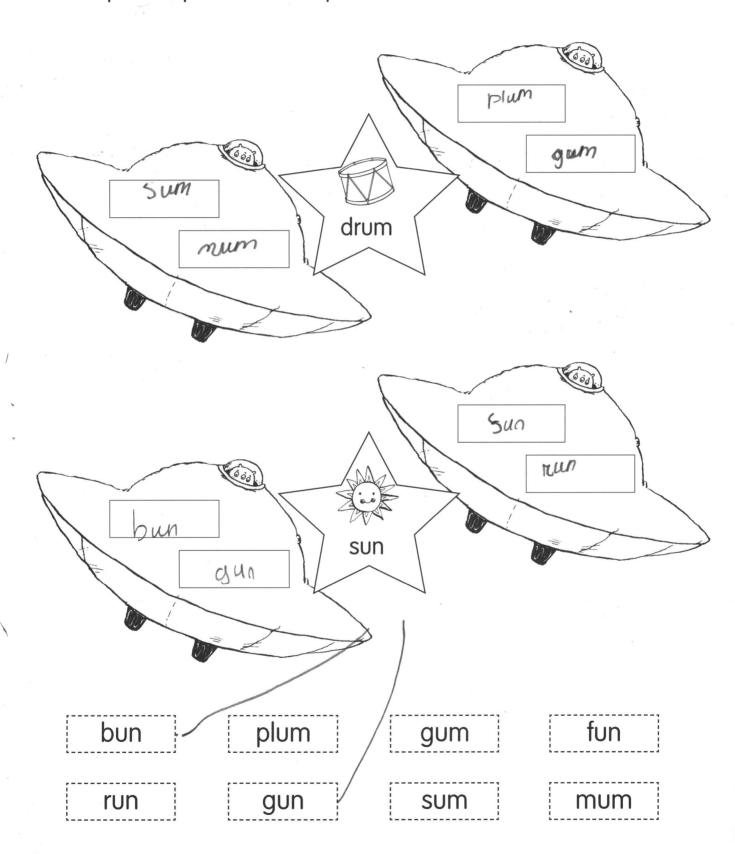

sum

mum

plum

gum

drum

bun

gun

Sun

run

sun

| bun | plum | gum | fun |
| run | gun | sum | mum |

Words that end in ld, nd and rd

Look at the pictures and say what they show. Blend the phonemes and say the words. Can you hear the phonemes at the ends of the words? Circle the correct word for each picture. Some of them are not real words.

★1 bald   band   bard

★2 hald   hand   hard

★3 cald   cand   card

★4 gold   gond   gord

★5 sald   sand   sard

★6 bild   bind   bird

38

Words that end in lk, nk and rk

Blend the phonemes to read the words at the bottom of the page. Look at the pictures and say what they show. Cut out the words and stick them by the pictures. One has been done for you.

walk

Fork

cork talk

wink

milk

kris

ark

cork

tank

trunk

trunk ✓	chalk ✓	✓ tank
cork ✓	ark ✓	✓ milk
sink ✓	fork ✓	✓ wink

Words that end in **lm** and **rm**

Blend the phonemes and read the sentences. Say the words in the boxes at the bottom of the page. Cut out the words and stick them in the correct sentences.

⭐ **1** There was no wind and the sea was | *calm* | .

⭐ **2** On the island there were lots of | *palm* | trees.

⭐ **3** Cows and sheep are | *farm* | animals.

⭐ **4** The fire | *alarm* | went off when I burnt my toast.

⭐ **5** The boat sank in the | *storm* | .

⭐ **6** A movie is the same as a | *silm* | .

| film | alarm | ~~calm~~ | ~~palm~~ | storm | farm |

⭐⭐⭐ ⭐ ⭐ ⭐ ⭐⭐ ⭐⭐⭐

Words that end in **lp**, **mp**, **rp** and **sp**

Blend the phonemes to read the words in the rockets. Write the words in the spaceships so that they rhyme.

help

elp

lamp

ump

camp

harp

stump

yelp

isp

amp

wisp

crisp

arp

sharp

thump

Words that end in ct, ft, lt, nt, rt and st

Read the words in the rockets. Can you hear the blends at the end of the words? Join the pairs of words which have the same final blends. One pair has been joined for you.

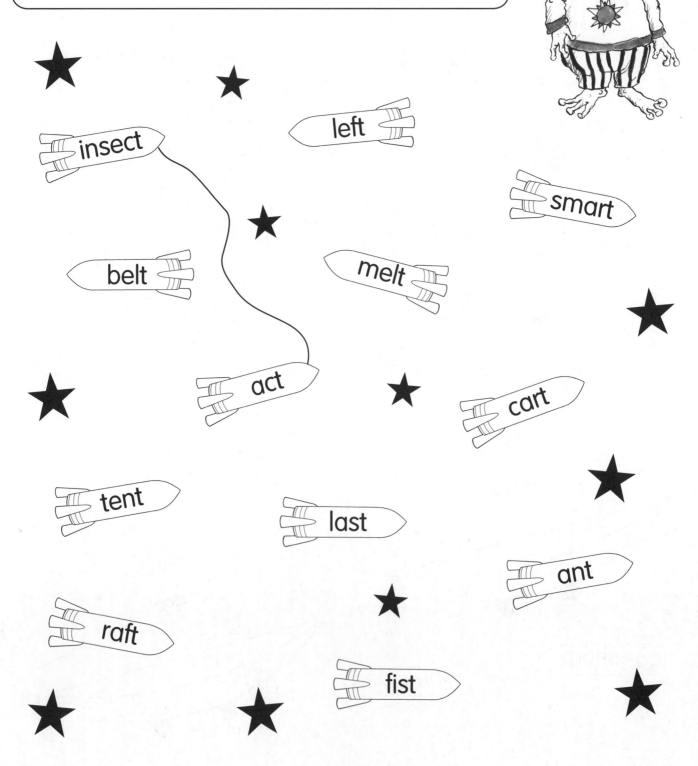

Words that end in nch, rch and tch

Look at the pictures and say what they show. Blend the phonemes to read the words in the planets. Can you hear the phonemes at the end of the word? Circle the correct picture for each word.

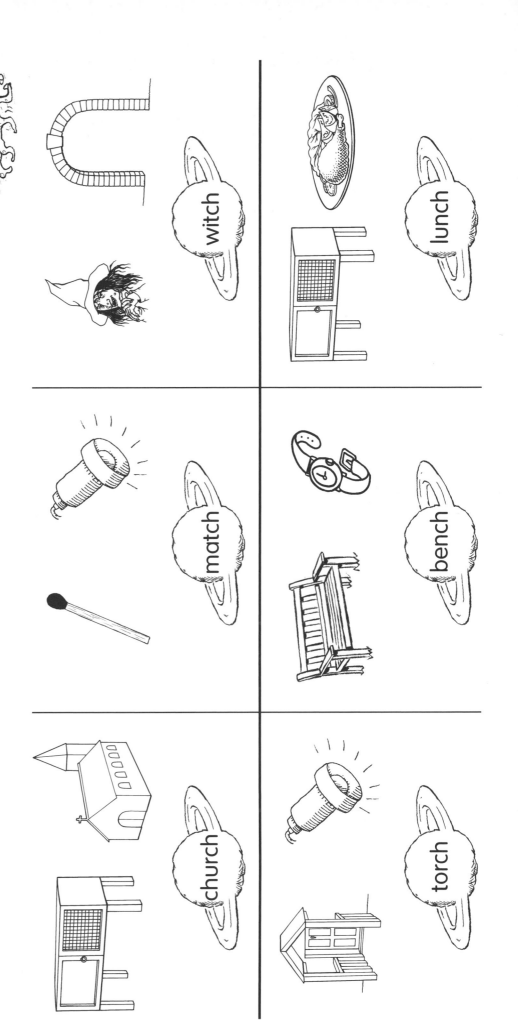

witch

lunch

match

bench

church

torch

Words that end in **ff, ll, ss, ck** and **ng**

Add the final phonemes to these letter strings and write the words on the lines. Use each ending twice. One has been done for you.

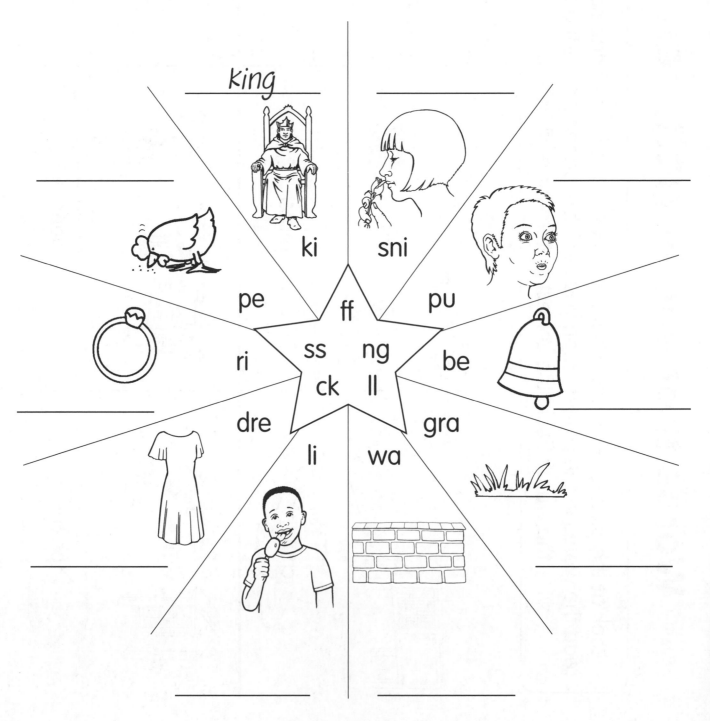

king

ki

sni

pe

pu

ff

ri

ss   ng

be

ck   ll

dre

gra

li   wa

44

Words that end in ck

Blend the phonemes to read the words in the word bank. Can you hear **ck** at the end of the words? Write the words in the pictures so that they rhyme.

Word bank

★ black   check   pack   suck   quick   pick   block   ★
rock   duck   shock   lick   snack   deck   neck   luck

sack

truck

wreck

sock

brick

Words that end in **ng**

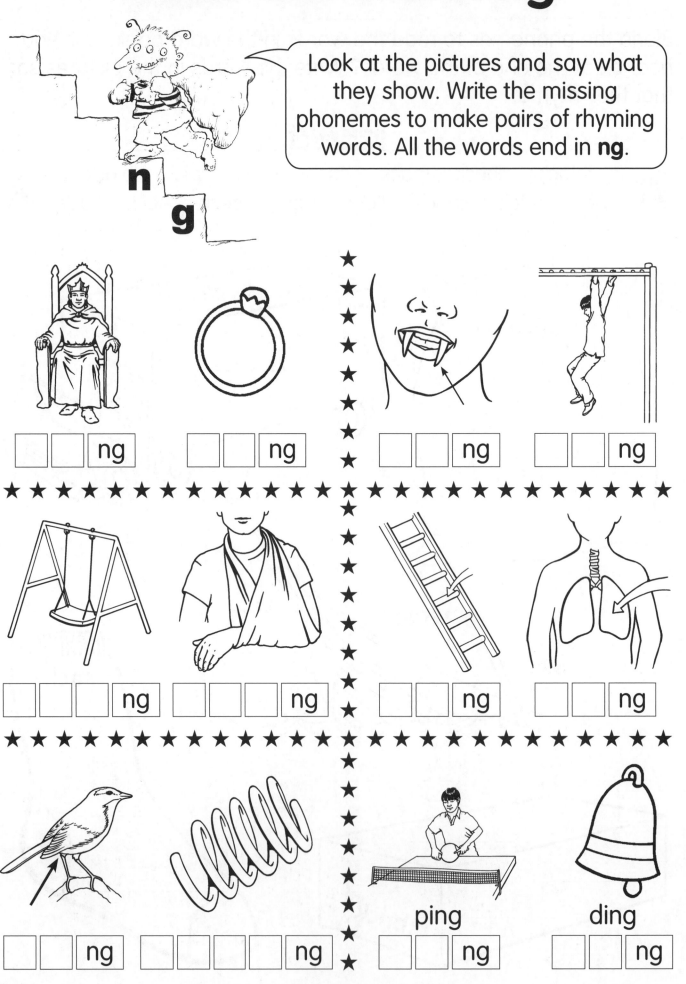

Look at the pictures and say what they show. Write the missing phonemes to make pairs of rhyming words. All the words end in **ng**.

☐ ☐ ng   ☐ ☐ ng   ☐ ☐ ng   ☐ ☐ ng

☐ ☐ ☐ ng   ☐ ☐ ☐ ng   ☐ ☐ ng   ☐ ☐ ng

☐ ☐ ng   ☐ ☐ ☐ ng   ping ☐ ☐ ng   ding ☐ ☐ ng

Hard and soft g

Blend the phonemes to read these words:

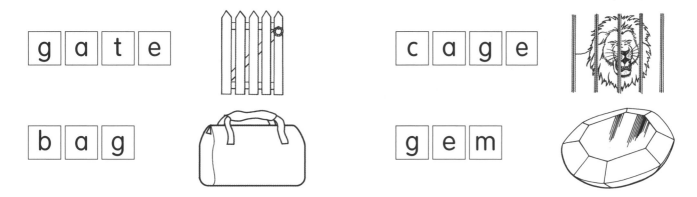

g a t e

b a g

c a g e

g e m

Can you hear the different **g** phonemes? The words *gate* and *bag* have a **hard g**. The words *cage* and *gem* have a **soft g**. This sounds like the phoneme **j**.

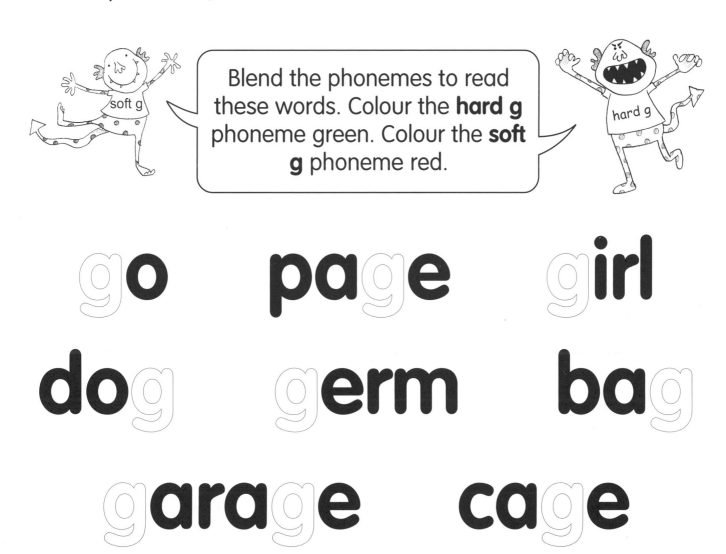

Blend the phonemes to read these words. Colour the **hard g** phoneme green. Colour the **soft g** phoneme red.

go   page   girl

dog   germ   bag

garage   cage

The ai phoneme spelt ay

The **ai** phoneme can be spelt **ay**, for example, *hay*, *say* and *may*.

Blend the phonemes to read the words in the word bank.
Write them in this rocket puzzle. Some letters have been
written in to help you. All the words end in **ay**.

Word bank

Friday   day   today
hay   say   away
play   lay   clay   way
Monday   pay

The **ai** phoneme

Blend the phonemes to read these words: *make, day* and *rain*. They are not spelt the same, but can you hear that they all have the **ai** phoneme? This phoneme can be spelt **ai**, **ay** and **a-e**.

Look at these pictures and read the words. Circle the pictures with the **ai** phoneme. Remember, it can be spelt **ai**, **ay** or **a-e**.

safe   rat   rain   pram   pray

sail   cape   tray   spade   cap

★ ★ ★ ★ ★ ★ ★ ★ ★ ★

Words that rhyme using the ai phoneme

Look at the letters in the wings of the alien insects. They spell words that rhyme. Use them to write two rhyming words on the lines below. Remember, the **ai** phoneme can be spelt **ai**, **ay** or **a-e**.

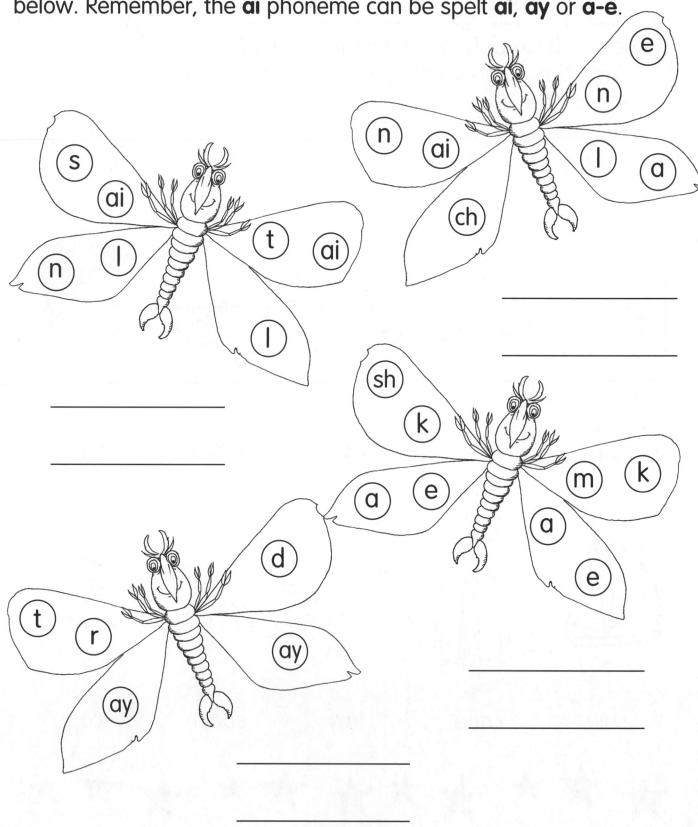

The ee phoneme

Blend the phonemes to read these words: *he, see* and *leaf*. They are not spelt the same but can you hear that they all have the **ee** phoneme? This phoneme can be spelt **ee**, **ea** or **e**.

Blend the phonemes to read these words. Colour the words with the **ee** phoneme. Remember, it can be spelt **ee**, **ea** or **e**. Be careful as some of the words are spelt with an **e** but do not have the **ee** phoneme.

bed she me

green neck

sea eat bee

week pet

Words that rhyme using the ee phoneme

Blend the phonemes to read the words at the bottom of the page. Look at the pictures and say what they show. Cut out the words and stick them around the picture that rhymes with the word. Words that rhyme are not always spelt in the same way.

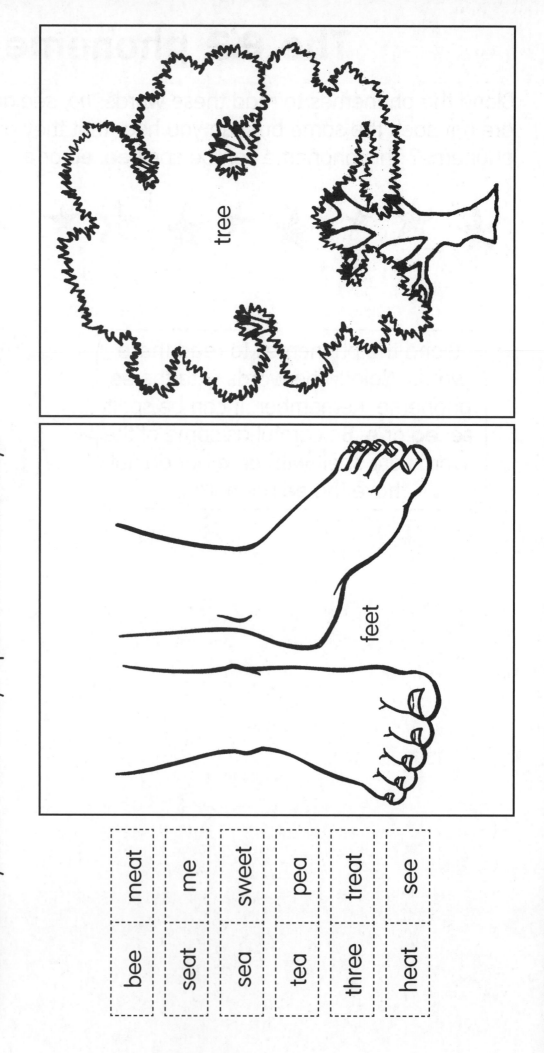

tree

feet

bee	meat
seat	me
sea	sweet
tea	pea
three	treat
heat	see

The **igh** phoneme

Blend the phonemes to read these words: *try, pie, line* and *sigh*.
They are not spelt the same but can you hear that they all have the
igh phoneme? This phoneme can be spelt **igh**, **y**, **ie** and **i-e**.

Blend the phonemes to read these letter
strings. Look at the pictures and say what
they show. Cut out the letter strings and
pictures. On a separate piece of paper, stick
the letter strings together to make words
with the **igh** phoneme. Stick the pictures
next to the words.

fr		ie	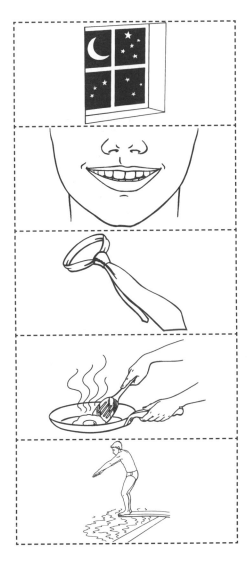
t		ight	
n	+	ile	
sm		y	
d		ive	

The **igh** phoneme

Blend the phonemes to read these words:

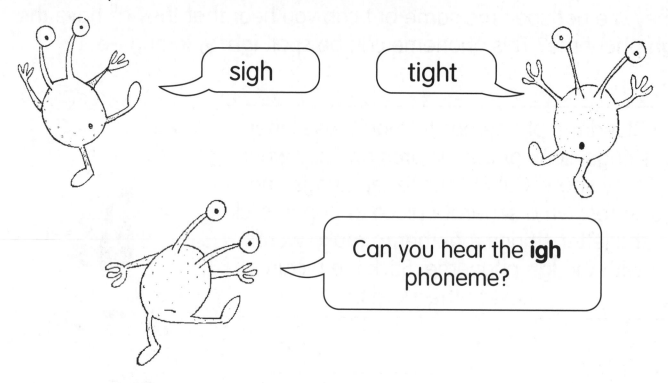

sigh

tight

Can you hear the **igh** phoneme?

Join these words to the pictures.

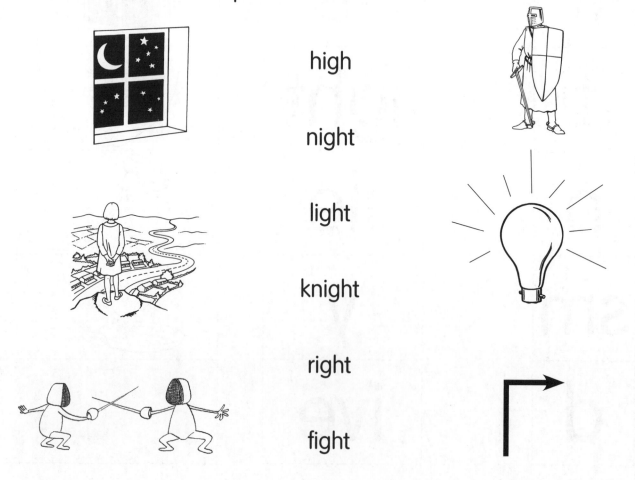

high

night

light

knight

right

fight

Words that rhyme using the igh phoneme

Read the word in the speech bubbles. In each letter puzzle there are four hidden words which rhyme with the word in the speech bubble. Circle the words. Words that rhyme do not have to be spelt in the same way.

The **oa** phoneme

Blend the phonemes to read these words: *no*, *low*, *home* and *foam*. They are not spelt the same but can you hear that they all have the **oa** phoneme? This phoneme can be spelt **oa**, **ow**, **o** or **o-e**.

Look at the pictures and say what they are. Use the phonemes to spell the words. Write them in the boxes.

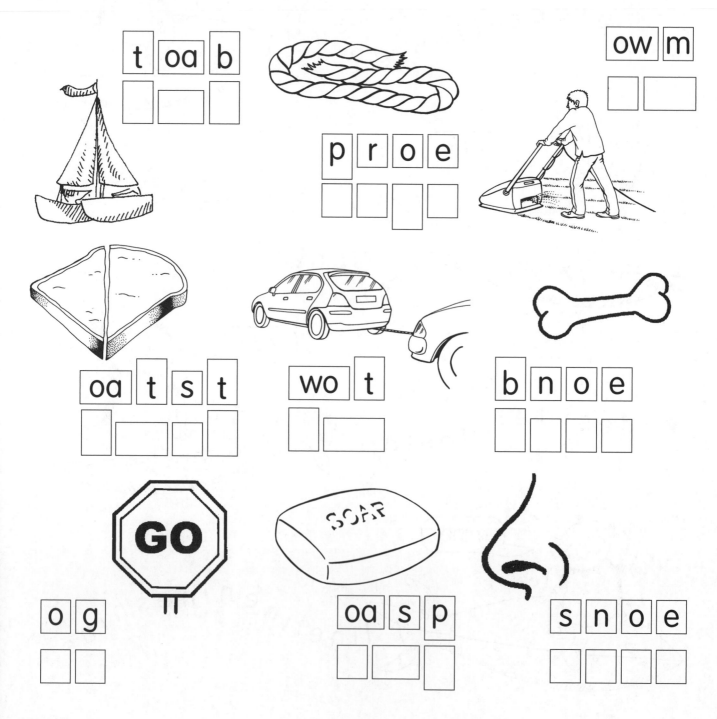

Words that rhyme using the oa phoneme

Look at the pictures. Blend the phonemes and say the words. Can you hear some words that rhyme? Write the words in the boxes in groups that rhyme.

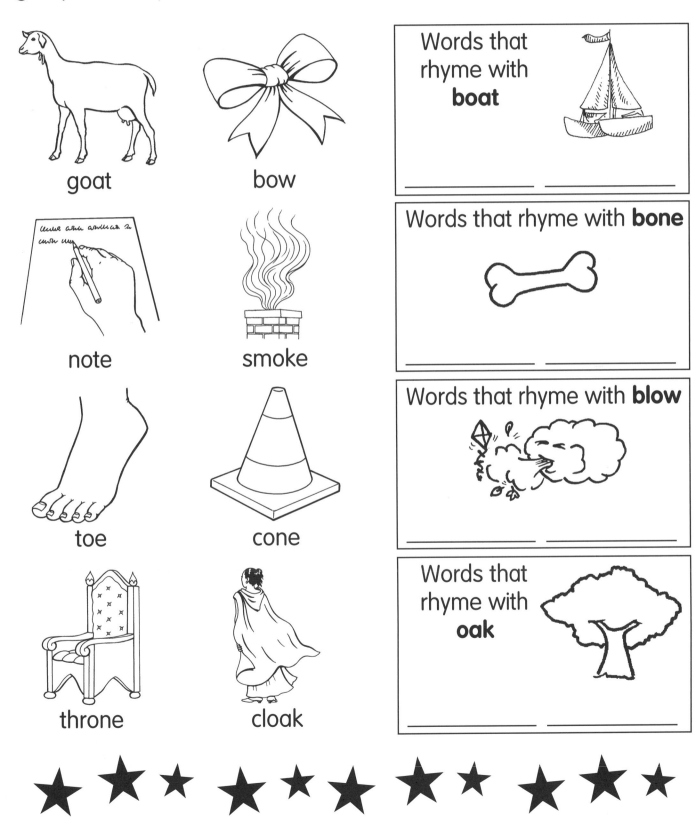

goat

bow

note

smoke

toe

cone

throne

cloak

Words that rhyme with **boat**

_____ _____

Words that rhyme with **bone**

_____ _____

Words that rhyme with **blow**

_____ _____

Words that rhyme with **oak**

_____ _____

The long OO phoneme

Blend the phonemes to read these words: *shoot, rule, blew* and *blue*. They are not spelt the same but can you hear that they have the same long **oo** phoneme? This can be spelt **oo**, **o-e**, **ew** or **ue**.

Join these phonemes together and write the words on the line. Then join them to the pictures.

| s | + | c | + | r | + | ew |

= _____

| m | + | oo | + | n |

= _____

| g | + | l | + | ue |

= _____

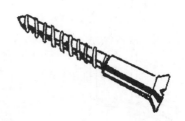

| sh | + | a | + | m | + | p | + | oo |

= _____

Words that rhyme using the long OO phoneme

Blend the phonemes to read the words.
Can you hear some words that rhyme?
Join the rhyming words together.
Remember, the rhyming words may
not be spelt in the same way.

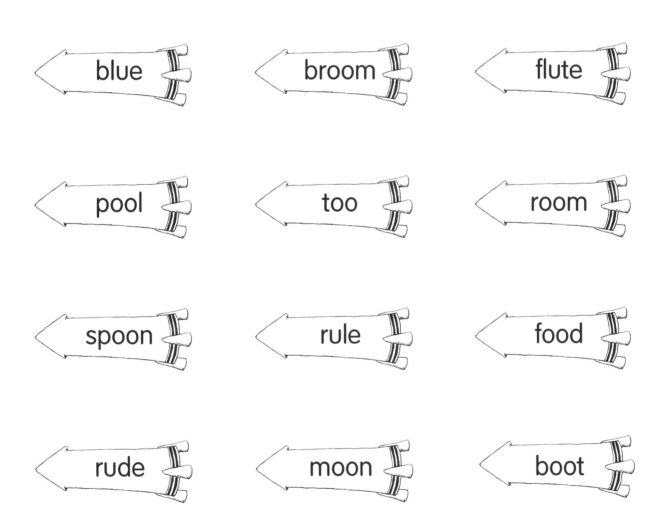

blue

broom

flute

pool

too

room

spoon

rule

food

rude

moon

boot

★ ★ ★ ★ ★ ★ ★ ★ ★ ★

Words with **ar**

Look at the pictures and say what they show. All these words have the phoneme **ar**. Choose the correct phonemes to complete the words. Write the words on the lines. Blend the phonemes to read the words.

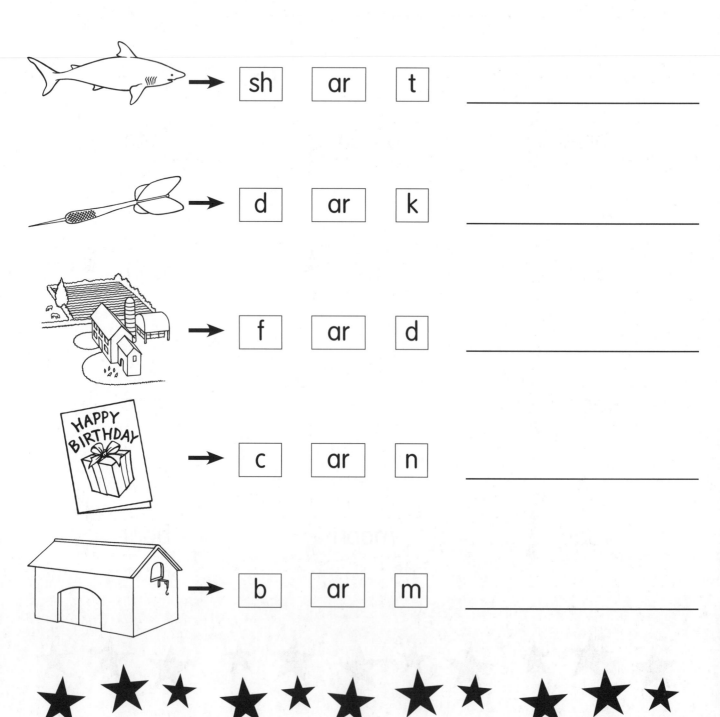

| sh | ar | t | _____ |

| d | ar | k | _____ |

| f | ar | d | _____ |

| c | ar | n | _____ |

| b | ar | m | _____ |

Words with aw

Blend the phonemes to read this word: *saw*. Can you hear the **aw** sound?

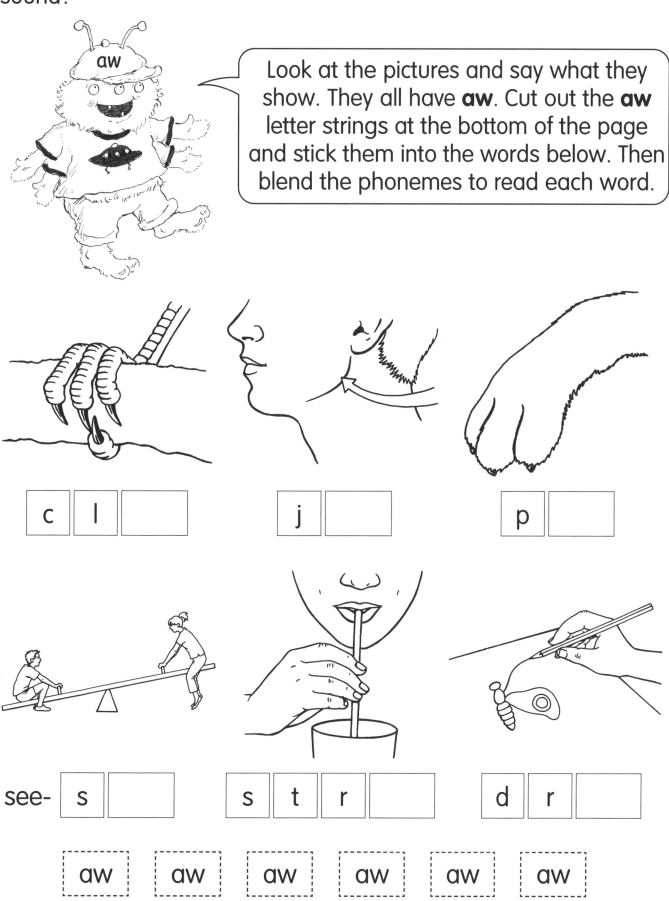

Look at the pictures and say what they show. They all have **aw**. Cut out the **aw** letter strings at the bottom of the page and stick them into the words below. Then blend the phonemes to read each word.

c l ☐   j ☐   p ☐

see- s ☐   s t r ☐   d r ☐

aw   aw   aw   aw   aw   aw

The Ur phoneme

Blend the phonemes and say these words: *her, girl* and *fur*. Can you hear the **ur** phoneme? It can be spelt **ur**, **er** or **ir**.

Choose the correct spelling of the phonemes for these words. Write the words on the lines. Blend the phonemes to read the words.

★1

b + | er |
    | ir | + d   = _____
    | ur |

★2

s + | er |
    | ir | + f   = _____
    | ur |

★3

f + | er |
    | ir | + n   = _____
    | ur |

★4

b + | er |
    | ir | + n   = _____
    | ur |

★5

sk + | er |
     | ir | + t = _____
     | ur |

Words with ea

Blend the phonemes to read these words: *sea* and *neat*. Can you hear the **ee** phoneme? This phoneme can be spelt **ea**.

Look at the pictures. Blend the phonemes to read the words. Colour the pictures with the **ee** phoneme spelt **ea**.

beads

meat

ice cream

bed

leaf

beak

beach

shed

peg

Words with air, are, ear and ere

Blend the phonemes to read these words:

h	air

c	are

b	ear

th	ere

Can you hear the **air** phoneme in these words? Can you see the different spellings? Look at the pictures and cut them out. Blend the phonemes to read the words at the bottom of the page and cut them out. Match the pictures to the words and stick them on a separate piece of paper.

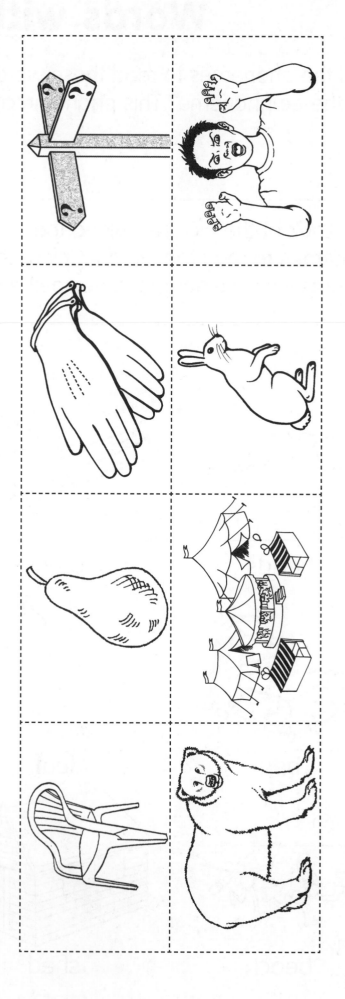

scare	pear	hare	chair	pair	where	bear	fair

Words with OW

Blend the phonemes to read these words:

| t | ow | n |

| s | l | ow |

Can you hear the difference?

Look at the pictures. Blend the phonemes to read the words. Colour those which rhyme with the **ow** phoneme in *town*. Circle those which rhyme with the **ow** phoneme in *slow*.

row

bow

elbow

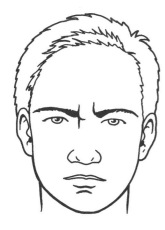

frown

crown

snow

Words with OO

Blend the phonemes to read these words: *good* and *room*. Can you hear the difference? Look at these pictures and read the words. Write words with a long **oo** phoneme in the pool and words with a short **oo** phoneme in the book.

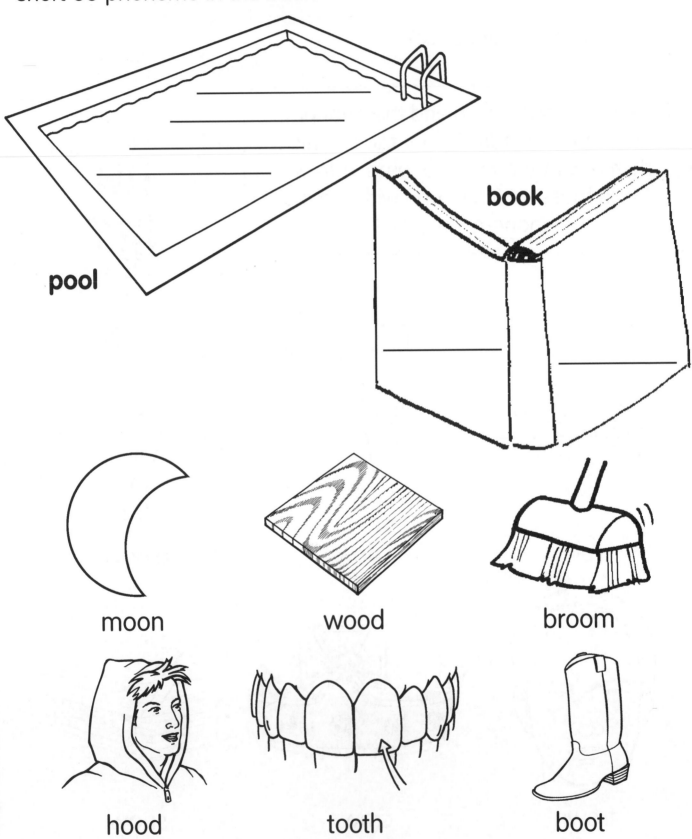

pool

book

moon

wood

broom

hood

tooth

boot

The oi phoneme

Blend the phonemes to read these words: *boy* and *coil*. The phoneme **oi** can be spelt **oy**.

★ ★ ★ ★ ★ ★ ★ ★ ★ ★

Blend the phonemes to read these words. Colour **oy** red. Colour **oi** blue.

toilet

toy

coin

soil

boy

The Or phoneme

Blend the phonemes to read these words: *for, floor* and *more*. The phoneme **or** can be spelt **or**, **oor** and **ore**.

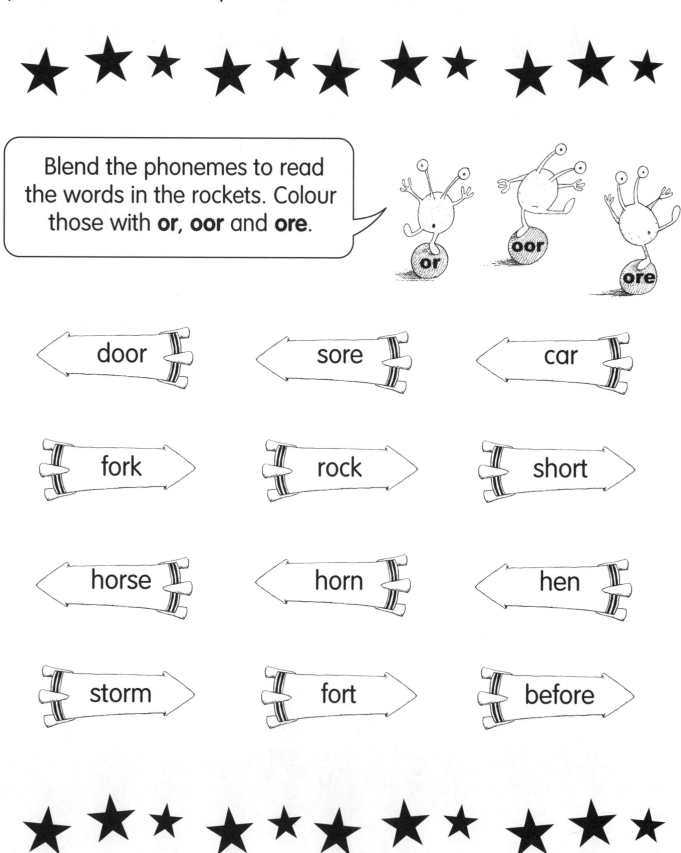

Blend the phonemes to read the words in the rockets. Colour those with **or**, **oor** and **ore**.

door

sore

car

fork

rock

short

horse

horn

hen

storm

fort

before

Plurals

Read the sentences. Change the words in the planets to plurals by adding **s,** for example, *brick – bricks*. Complete the sentences.

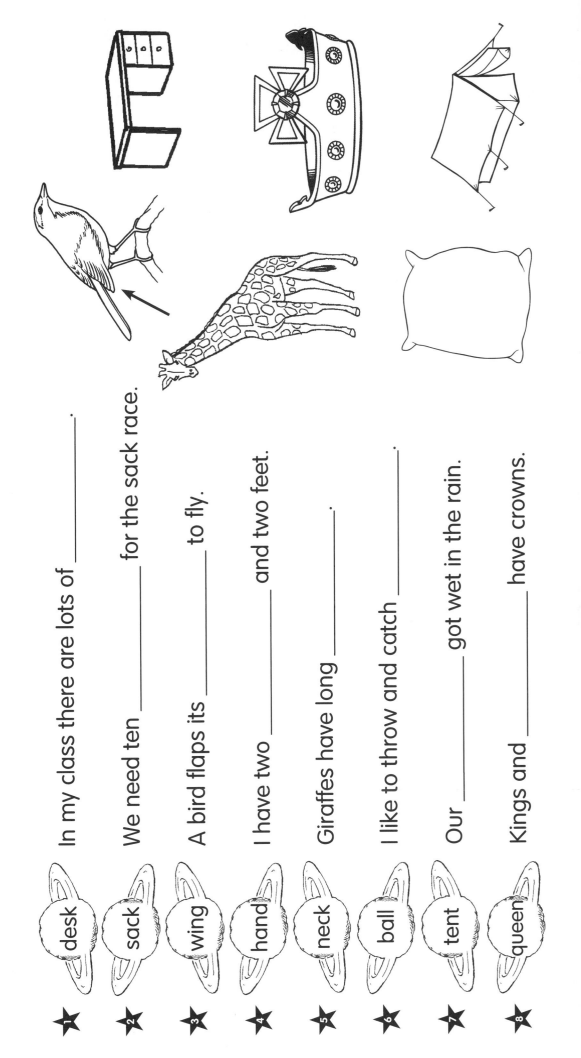

⭐1 In my class there are lots of _____ .

⭐2 We need ten _____ for the sack race.

⭐3 A bird flaps its _____ to fly.

⭐4 I have two _____ and two feet.

⭐5 Giraffes have long _____ .

⭐6 I like to throw and catch _____ .

⭐7 Our _____ got wet in the rain.

⭐8 Kings and _____ have crowns.

desk

sack

wing

hand

neck

ball

tent

queen

Adding ed

Read this sentence: *Last week I bumped my head.* Can you see that the word *bump* has **ed** on the end?

★ ★ ★ ★ ★ ★ ★ ★ ★ ★ ★

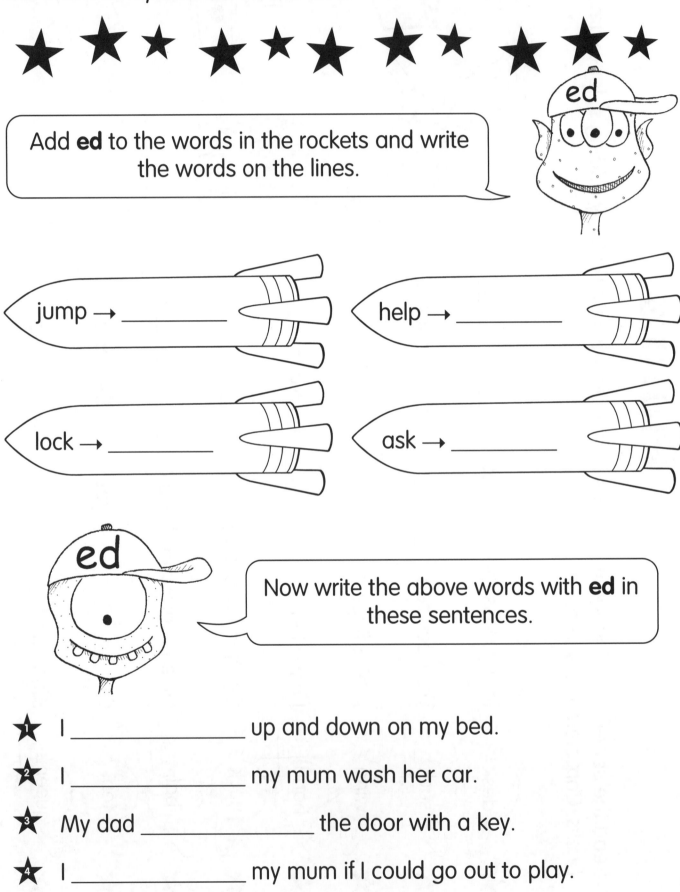

Add **ed** to the words in the rockets and write the words on the lines.

jump → _____

help → _____

lock → _____

ask → _____

Now write the above words with **ed** in these sentences.

★ I _____ up and down on my bed.

★2 I _____ my mum wash her car.

★3 My dad _____ the door with a key.

★4 I _____ my mum if I could go out to play.

Adding ing

Read this sentence: *I am going home soon.* Can you see that the word *go* has **ing** on the end?

★ ★ ★ ★ ★ ★ ★ ★ ★ ★ ★

Add **ing** to the words in the spaceships and write the words on the lines.

ing

kick
_____

sink
_____

walk
_____

jump
_____

Words that end in y

Blend the phonemes to read these words: *hairy* and *teddy*. Can you hear the phoneme **ee** at the end? This phoneme can be spelt with a **y**.

Blend the phonemes to read the words in the spaceship. Join each word to a picture.

fairy   puppy

baby   cherry   teddy

dirty

Words with double letters

Blend the phonemes to read these words: *letter, correct* and *running*. They have two letters in the middle which are the same.

★ ★ ★ ★ ★ ★ ★ ★ ★ ★ ★

Look at the pictures and say what they show. Write the double letters from the box below in the middle of each word. The last word has no picture clue to help you!

| ★ | tt | pp | mm | nn | ff | bb | ★ |

1 ho __ __ ing

2 bu __ __ on

3 to __ __ ee

4 ke __ __ el

5 ro __ __ er

6 su __ __ er

★ ★ ★ ★ ★ ★ ★ ★ ★ ★ ★

Words with er

Blend the phonemes to read these words: *louder, sweeter, teacher* and *singer*. Can you hear **er** at the end of each word?

Blend the phonemes to read the words in the rockets. Break them up as in the example.

Example: jumper = | jump | + | er |

duster = | | + | |

quicker = | | + | |

cracker = | | + | |

older = | | + | |

taller = | | + | |

walker = | | + | |

recorder = | | + | |

Words with ly

Blend the phonemes to read these words: *sweetly* and *loudly*. Can you hear **ly** at the end of each word?

Read the letters and letter strings below. Choose a letter or letter string from each rocket to spell words that end in **ly**. Write them on the lines. One has been done as an example.

n
s
qu
n
b
gl
n
s

ick
ad
ice
ad
eat
um
oft
ear

nicely

+ ly _____

Syllables

Blend the phonemes to read these words: *rib, ribbon* and *robbery*.
Can you hear how many syllables each word has?

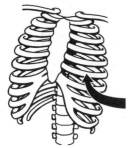

rib = 1 syllable   ribbon = 2 syllables   robbery = 3 syllables

Write your first name on the line. _____

How many syllables does your first name have? _____

Write your last name on the line. _____

How many syllables does your last name have? _____

Write the number of syllables of the
words below in the stars.

this   = ☆   Saturday = ☆   yellow   = ☆

mother   = ☆   name   = ☆   garden   = ☆

door   = ☆   suddenly = ☆   light   = ☆

morning = ☆   window   = ☆   ball   = ☆

Compound words

Blend the phonemes to read these words:

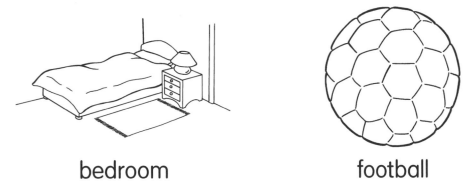

bedroom   football

Can you hear the two small words that make the big word?

Blend the phonemes to read the small words in the table below.
Join them together to write a big word. Cut out the pictures and
stick them next to the words.

Small words	Big word	Picture
cow + boy		
ear + ring		
toe + nail		
jelly + fish		
scare + crow		

Things at school (nouns)

Blend the phonemes to read the words. Look at the picture. Cut out the words and stick them on the picture in the correct places.

pen	chair
door	book
girl	ball
desk	table
window	light
boy	bat

Things in the garden (nouns)

Blend the phonemes to read the words. Look at the picture. Cut out the words and stick them on the picture in the correct places.

dog	gate
peg	roof
bin	pond
cat	flower
slug	tree
snail	path
sun	grass

Opposites (antonyms)

Blend the phonemes to read these words: *hot – cold*. These words have opposite meanings and are called **antonyms**. Blend the phonemes to read the words below. Cut out the words at the bottom of the page and stick them next to their opposites.

short

fast

fat

old

dry

★ sad
★
★
★ him
★
★
★ hard
★
★
★ first
★
★
★ small

| tall | thin | big | slow | her |
| happy | soft | wet | new | last |

Words with un and dis

Blend the phonemes to read these sentences:

I am happy, but he is unhappy.
I like jam but I dislike butter.

Can you see that the words *happy* and *like* have **un** and **dis** in front of them? The letter strings **un** and **dis** make the words mean the opposite. Add **un** and **dis** to these words and write them on the lines.

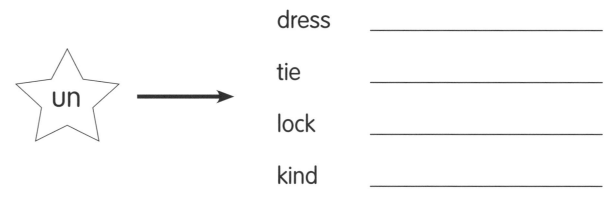

dress   _____

tie   _____

lock   _____

kind   _____

★ ★

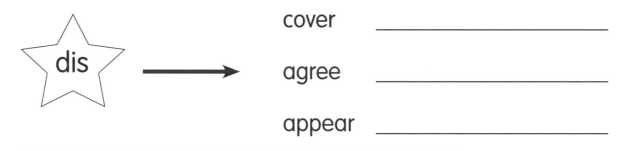

cover   _____

agree   _____

appear   _____

Circle the correct words in these sentences.

★ I **undress/unkind** when I have a bath.
★ To take off my shoes I **unlock/untie** the laces.
★ We **unhappy/unlock** the door to get in.
★ The ugly sisters were **unkind/untie** to Cinderella.
★ The aliens wanted to **disagree/discover** new planets.
★ My sister and I always **disagree/disappear**.

High frequency words

Blend the phonemes to read the words in the walls. Write the words in the word grids. Look at the letters in the words carefully to see where they will fit. Some letters have been written in the grids to help you. Find the hidden word shaded in each grid and write it in on the line.

Hidden word: _____

Hidden word: _____

Hidden word: _____

High frequency words in sentences

Read the sentences. Write the missing words in the gaps. The words you need are in the rockets.

⭐ 1 My mum _____ I are _____ to the shops.

going   and

⭐ 2 I _____ to go fishing with _____ dad.

like   my

⭐ 3 You must _____ left and right when _____ cross the road.

look   you

⭐ 4 My dad _____ 'Go and _____ in the park.'

said   play

⭐ 5 We _____ to the beach _____ a holiday.

for   went

⭐ 6 I _____ see the _____ dog.

big   can

⭐ 7 Can you _____ the cat _____ the tree?

up   see

⭐ 8 We _____ going to _____ wet in the rain.

get   are

⭐ 9 She _____ sad and so were _____.

they   was

⭐ 10 My dad said, '_____ and look at _____.'

this   come

83

High frequency words – how many letters?

Read the words in the word bank. Find and circle them in the wordsearch. The words can only be read across, not up or down.

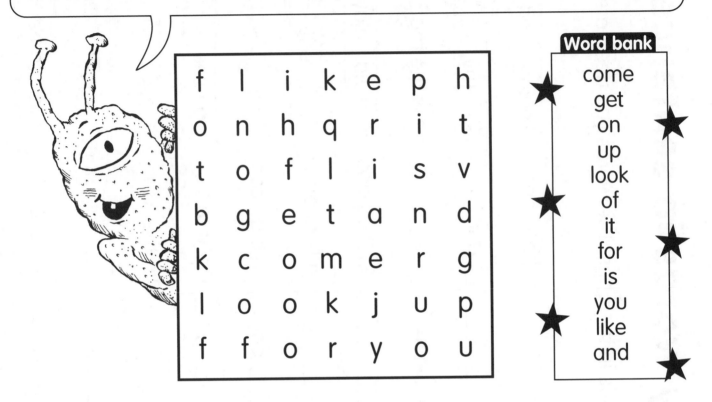

Word bank

come
get
on
up
look
of
it
for
is
you
like
and

Count the numbers of letters in each word in the word bank and sort them into the rockets below. One of each has been done for you.

2 letters
on

3 letters
for

4 letters
look

Sorting high frequency words by first phoneme

Blend the phonemes to read the words in the word bank. Find and circle them in the wordsearch. The words can only be read across and down.

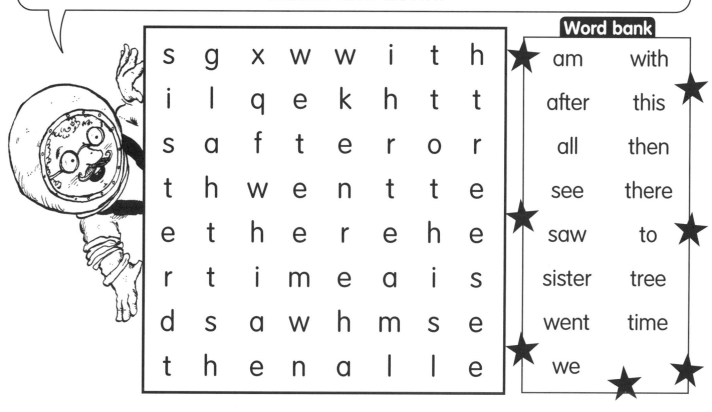

Word bank

am	with
after	this
all	then
see	there
saw	to
sister	tree
went	time
we	

Wordsearch:

s	g	x	w	w	i	t	h
i	l	q	e	k	h	t	t
s	a	f	t	e	r	o	r
t	h	w	e	n	t	t	e
e	t	h	e	r	e	h	e
r	t	i	m	e	a	i	s
d	s	a	w	h	m	s	e
t	h	e	n	a	l	l	e

Look at the first phoneme of each word in the word bank and write them in the correct boxes below. The first one has been done for you.

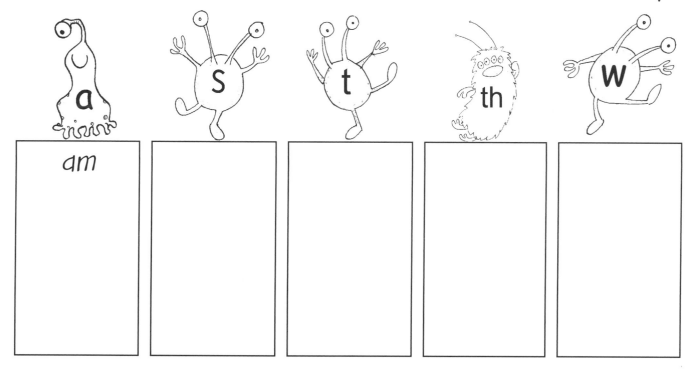

a	s	t	th	w
am				

What can aliens do? (verbs)

We can do lots of things. What can aliens do? Blend the phonemes to read the words in the rockets. They are 'doing' words which are called **verbs**. Join each word to the alien who is doing what it says.

How do aliens feel? (adjectives)

Blend the phonemes to read the words in the word bank. How do aliens feel? Look at the pictures and the words in the word bank. Write the words in the boxes beside the pictures. The first one has been done for you.

Word bank

hot   sad   sleepy   mad   happy   cold

hot

Upper and lower case letters

These are the upper case letters of the alphabet. They are also called capital letters.

A B C D E F G H I J K L M N O P Q R S T U V W X Y

These are the lower case letters of the alphabet

a b c d e f g h i j k l m n o p q r s t u v w x y

The letters below are in pairs. Write the missing upper or lower case letters in the stars to make pairs of letters.

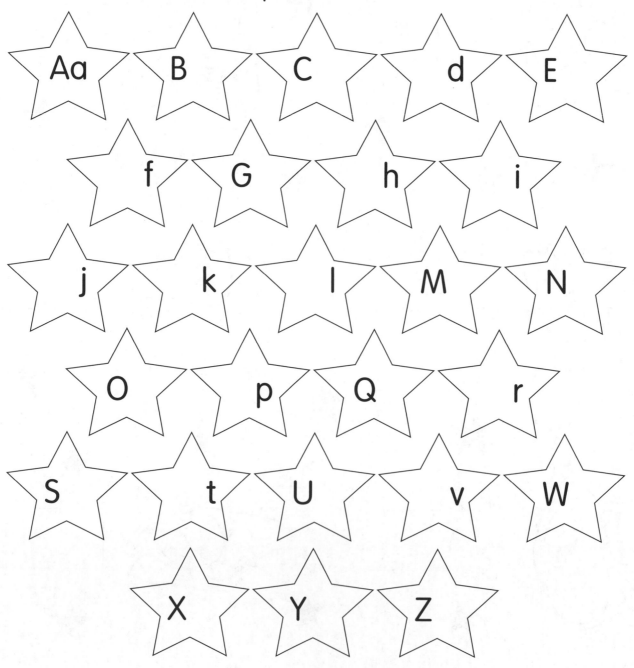

Upper case letters

Capital letters are used for names of people, places, days of the week and months of the year. Circle the capital letters for the seven days of the week and write the missing phoneme for each day of the week next to it. Make sure that you use capital letters. Then do the same for the months of the year.

Days of the week

★ ★ ★ ★ ★ ★ ★ ★ ★ ★ ★ ★ ★ ★ ★ ★ ★ ★ ★ ★

Monday   [ ] onday

Tuesday   [ ] uesday

Wednesday   [ ] ednesday

Thursday   [ ] hursday

Friday   [ ] riday

Saturday   [ ] aturday

Sunday   [ ] unday

Months of the year

January   [ ] anuary   July   [ ] uly

February   [ ] ebruary   August   [ ] ugust

March   [ ] arch   September   [ ] eptember

April   [ ] pril   October   [ ] ctober

May   [ ] ay   November   [ ] ovember

June   [ ] une   December   [ ] ecember

Answers

■ PAGE 5

be**d** rub **b**lack	hen hat hop
cat cut cub	jam jog jet
dog bed drum	leg ball clap
fox fat flag	mop jam plum
go bug green	nut hen run

■ PAGE 6

peg cup pit	vet vest have
queen quick quack	wet we went
rat rain tree	box fix fox
sun yes sail	yes yelp you
tap pet trip	zip zoo zebra

■ PAGE 7

ant bag ran mat
red bed met net
in pig dig win
on pot hot stop
up bug drum lump

■ PAGE 8

a b c d e f g h i j k l m n o p q r s t u v w x y z

■ PAGE 9

a b c d e f g
h i j k l m n o
p q r s t
u v w x y z

a b c d e f g h i j k l m n o p q r s t u v w x y z

■ PAGE 10

def
ghi
jkl
mno

■ PAGE 11

pqr
stu
vwx
yz

■ PAGE 12

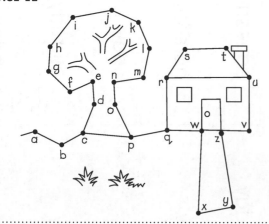

■ PAGE 13

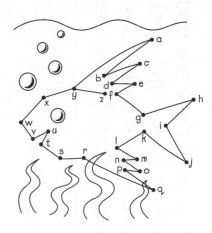

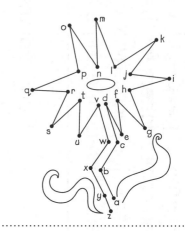

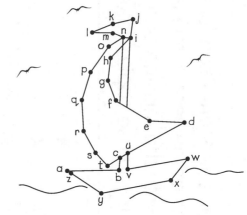

■ PAGE 14

bed	pin
cat	six
fox	ten
hen	umbrella
jug	web
leg	yacht
map	zip

■ PAGE 15

bat	net
cup	rat
fan	sun
hat	vest
mop	wig

■ **PAGE 16**

blow

glue

claw

plug

flag

slug

■ **PAGE 17**

crab

pram

drum

train

grin

frog

■ **PAGE 18**

| twins | swan | swing | dwarf | swim | twelve |

twins

dwarf

swan

swim

swing

twelve **12**

■ **PAGE 19**

1. The cut on my leg left a bad (scar).
2. I like to (skip) to keep fit.
3. Some flowers (smell) nice.
4. A good card game is (snap).
5. It is very rude to (spit).
6. The bus (stop) is next to the shop.

scar
skip
smell

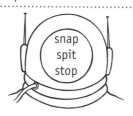

snap
spit
stop

■ **PAGE 20**

1. My cut began to **bleed**.
2. Mud is **brown**.
3. I like strawberries and **cream**.
4. He was a funny **clown**.
5. Catch the ball, don't **drop** it.
6. Birds can **fly**.
7. My painting had a red **frame**.
8. The fire began to **glow**.
9. My plant **grew** tall.
10. The princess was **pretty**.

■ **PAGE 21**

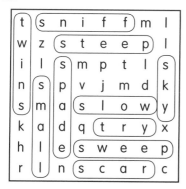

t	s	n	i	f	f	m	l
w	z	s	t	e	e	p	l
i	l	s	m	p	t	l	s
n	s	p	v	j	m	d	k
s	m	a	s	l	o	w	y
k	a	d	q	t	r	y	a
h	l	e	s	w	e	e	p
r	l	n	s	c	a	r	c

■ **PAGE 22**

1. I **chew** food with my teeth.
   My dog likes to **chase** cats.
2. I put the tins on the **shelf**.
   The **shop** sells ice creams.
3. I said **thank** you for the gifts.
   The old dog was very **thin**.
4. After my swim, I had a hot **shower**.
   The sun made a big **shadow** under the tree.
5. My **cheeks** were red with sunburn.
   Our teacher writes with **chalk**.

■ **PAGE 23**

screen   scrub
scratch   splash
scream   split

■ **PAGE 24**

spray   spring   square   squirt

■ **PAGE 25**

straw   strong
street   strawberry
string   stretch

■ **PAGE 26**

1. screw   4. string
2. splash   5. splint
3. scrub   6. spring

■ **PAGE 27**

three **3**

thrush

throne

throw

■ **PAGE 28**

th	r	i	l	l
th	r	u	sh
th	r	ow
th	r	ee
sh	r	u	b
sh	r	i	e	k
sh	r	u	g
sh	r	i	n	k

■ PAGE 29

1. I had a small **scrap** of paper to write my name on.
2. The **stray** dog had no home.
3. We had to **squash** the clothes into the small case.
4. The fish were in the **stream**.
5. I had to **thread** the needle to sew.
6. I **threw** the ball into the net.
7. He had a **splinter** of wood in his finger.
8. She jumps up and down as if she is on **springs**.
9. I **spread** the jam on my toast.
10. The mouse made my mum **scream**.

■ PAGE 30

white	ele**ph**ant	**wh**en
chorus	**wh**ip	**wh**eel
whale	**ph**oto	tele**ph**one

■ PAGE 31

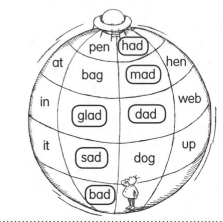

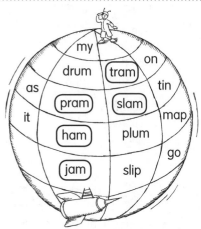

■ PAGE 32

can	clap	hat
plan	cap	cat
fan	trap	bat

■ PAGE 33

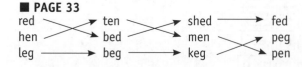

■ PAGE 34

ip	in	it
pip	pin	pit
sip	bin	sit
nip	sin	bit
hip		hit
		nit

■ PAGE 35

dog	dot
log	cot
jog	pot
fog	hot

■ PAGE 36

shop	plug
top	bug
mop	jug
chop	mug

■ PAGE 37

drum	sun
plum	gun
gum	bun
mum	run
sum	fun

■ PAGE 38

1. bald	4. gold
2. hand	5. sand
3. card	6. bird

■ PAGE 39

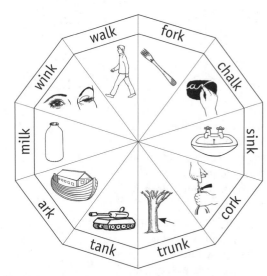

■ PAGE 40

1. There was no wind and the sea was **calm**.
2. On the island there were lots of **palm** trees.
3. Cows and sheep are **farm** animals.
4. The fire **alarm** went off when I burnt my toast.
5. The boat sank in the **storm**.
6. A movie is the same as a **film**.

■ PAGE 41

elp	ump	amp	isp	arp
help	stump	camp	wisp	sharp
yelp	thump	lamp	crisp	harp

■ **PAGE 42**

insect – act   belt – melt
left – raft   tent – ant
smart – cart   fist – last

■ **PAGE 43**

church    torch

match   bench

witch   lunch

■ **PAGE 44**

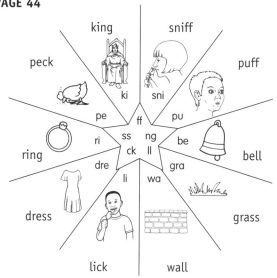

king   sniff
peck   puff
ki   sni
pe   ff   pu
ring   ri ss ng be   bell
ck ll
dre   gra
li   wa
dress   grass
lick   wall

■ **PAGE 45**

sack	truck	wreck	sock	brick
black	suck	neck	rock	lick
pack	duck	check	block	pick
snack	luck	deck	shock	quick

■ **PAGE 46**

king – ring   rung – lung
fang – hang   ping pong – ding dong
wing – spring   swing – sling

■ **PAGE 47**

Hard g phoneme	Soft g phoneme
go	page
girl	gara**g**e
dog	cage
garage	germ
bag	

■ **PAGE 48**

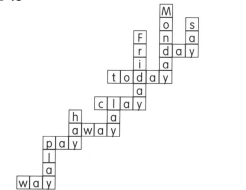

■ **PAGE 49**

safe   sail
rain   tray
pray   spade

■ **PAGE 50**

snail – tail   shake – make
chain – lane   tray – day

■ **PAGE 51**

green   she   me   sea   week   eat   bee

■ **PAGE 52**

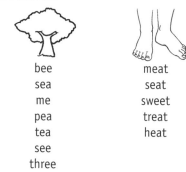

bee   meat
sea   seat
me   sweet
pea   treat
tea   heat
see
three

■ **PAGE 53**

fry    smile

tie   dive

night

■ **PAGE 54**

high   knight

night   right

light   fight

■ **PAGE 55**

dry – pie cry tie high
kite – night bite white fight
ride – wide side tide hide
mine – line fine nine shine

■ **PAGE 56**

boat   bone

rope   go

mow   soap

toast   nose

tow

■ **PAGE 57**

boat	bone	blow	oak
goat	cone	bow	smoke
note	throne	toe	cloak

■ PAGE 58

screw   glue

moon   shampoo

■ PAGE 59

blue – too   spoon – moon
pool – rule   rude – food
broom – room   boot – flute

■ PAGE 60

 shark   card

 dart   barn

 farm

■ PAGE 61

claw   see-saw

jaw   straw

paw   draw

■ PAGE 62

bird
surf
fern
burn
skirt

■ PAGE 63

beads   leaf
meat   beak
ice cream   beach

■ PAGE 64

 chair   hare

 pear   where

 pair   scare

 bear   fair

■ PAGE 65

town: frown, crown, bow.
slow: row, elbow, snow.

■ PAGE 66

pool: moon, tooth, boot, broom.
book: wood, hood.

■ PAGE 67

oy: toy, boy.
oi: coin, point, toilet, soil.

■ PAGE 68

door
sore
fork
short

horse
horn
storm
fort
before

■ PAGE 69

1. In my class there are lots of **desks**.
2. We need ten **sacks** for the sack race.
3. A bird flaps its **wings** to fly.
4. I have two **hands** and two feet.
5. Giraffes have long **necks**.
6. I like to throw and catch **balls**.
7. Our **tents** got wet in the rain.
8. Kings and **queens** have crowns.

■ PAGE 70

jumped
helped
locked
asked

1. I **jumped** up and down on my bed.
2. I **helped** my mum wash her car.
3. My dad **locked** the door with a key.
4. I **asked** my mum if I could go out to play.

■ PAGE 71

sinking
kicking
walking
jumping

■ PAGE 72

fairy   cherry

baby   puppy

dirty   teddy

■ PAGE 73

1. hopping
2. button
3. toffee
4. kennel
5. robber
6. summer

■ PAGE 74

jumper = jump + er   older = old + er
duster = dust + er   taller = tall + er
quicker = quick + er   walker = walk + er
cracker = crack + er   recorder = record + er

■ PAGE 75

nicely   badly
sadly/softly/sickly   glumly
quickly   nearly/neatly
neatly/nearly   softly/sadly

■ PAGE 76

this = 1   Saturday = 3   yellow = 2
mother = 2   name = 1   garden = 2
door = 1   suddenly = 3   light = 1
morning = 2   window = 2   ball = 1

cowboy

jellyfish

earring

scarecrow

toenail

■ PAGE 78

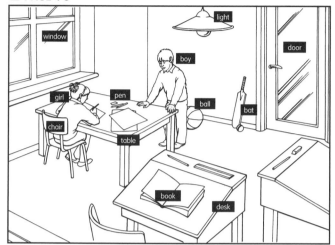

light · window · boy · door · girl · pen · ball · bat · chair · table · book · desk

■ PAGE 79

roof · sun · cat · gate · bin · dog · tree · flower · path · grass · slug · pond · peg · snail

■ PAGE 80

short – tall	sad – happy
fast – slow	him – her
fat – thin	hard – soft
old – new	first – last
dry – wet	small – big

■ PAGE 81

undress
untie
unlock
unkind

....

discover
disagree
disappear

....

1. I **undress** when I have a bath.
2. To take off my shoes I **untie** the laces.
3. We **unlock** the door to get in.
4. The ugly sisters were **unkind** to Cinderella.
5. The aliens wanted to **discover** new planets.
6. My sister and I always **disagree**.

■ PAGE 82

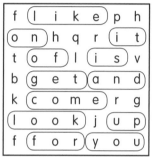

■ PAGE 83

1. My mum **and** I are **going** to the shops.
2. I **like** to go fishing with **my** dad.
3. You must **look** left and right when **you** cross the road.
4. My dad **said**, 'Go and **play** in the park.'
5. We **went** to the beach **for** a holiday.
6. I **can** see the **big** dog.
7. Can you **see** the cat **up** the tree?
8. We **are** going to **get** wet in the rain.
9. She **was** sad and so were **they**.
10. My dad said, '**Come** and look at **this**.'

■ PAGE 84

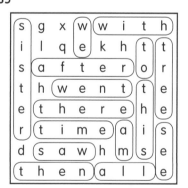

2 letters	3 letters	4 letters
on	for	look
is	get	like
up	you	come
of	and	
it		

■ PAGE 85

a	s	t	th	w
am	see	to	this	went
all	saw	tree	then	we
after	sister	time	there	with

96